Developing and Implementing
Knowledge Management
in the Parliament of Finland

Developing and Implementing Knowledge Management in the Parliament of Finland

Riitta Suurla,
Markku Markkula
and
Olli Mustajärvi

The Committee for the Future / Steering Group of the Technology Assessment Project:
Markku Markkula (chair), Anne Huotari, Susanna Huovinen, Kyösti Karjula,
Riitta Korhonen and Irina Krohn.

Steering Group and project teams' chairpersons of the Information Systems and Knowledge Management Project: Keijo Koivukangas (chair), Kari T. Ahonen, Markku Markkula,
Jouni Vainio, Ari Apilo, Marita Hänninen, Olli Mustajärvi and Antti Rautava.

For additional information, please contact:

Markku Markkula, Member of Parliament
The Parliament of Finland
FIN-00102 HELSINKI, FINLAND
Phone: +358 50 5113146
E-mail: markku.markkula@eduskunta.fi

Olli Mustajärvi, Head of IT Office
The Parliament of Finland
FIN-00102 HELSINKI, FINLAND
Phone: +358 9 432 2583
E-mail: olli.mustajarvi@eduskunta.fi

Ulrica Gabrielsson, Researcher
The Committee for the Future
The Parliament of Finland
FIN-00102 HELSINKI, FINLAND
Phone: +358 9 4322183
E-mail:ulrica.gabrielsson@eduskunta.fi

Riitta Suurla, Managing Director
Taitoakatemia Oy
Vanha Rantatie 394 C 25
FIN-02420 JORVAS, FINLAND
Phone: +358 40 5905149
E-mail: riitta.suurla@taito.pp.fi

ISBN 951-53-2413-0 (Print)
ISBN 951-53-2414-9 (Pdf)

Edita Prima Oy
Helsinki, Finland, 2002

Foreword

Through globalisation and complex work processes, innovation has become an increasingly crucial success factor for individuals, businesses, other communities and society. It was 5 years ago that the Parliament of Finland, while analysing Finland's future prospects, highlighted innovation, with special emphasis on its human aspects, as one of the four all-permeating success factors. The Committee for the Future has comprehensively investigated innovation. Innovation is not an automatic process. It requires a change of attitude and a high-quality context for the methods to develop.

With respect to these challenges and opportunities knowledge management plays a crucial role.

Knowledge management means discovery learning. Knowledge management is an issue which involves the wise care and development of knowledge, skills and communication based on a desired and shared vision of the future. Knowledge management is based on jointly defined values. Knowledge management requires innovative, responsible leadership.

The above is a definition that we arrived at as a Technology Assessment Project's (TA Project) Steering Group that consisted of Members of Parliament representing various parliamentary committees and political parties. This definition shows that knowledge management includes many dimensions.

Our first intention through this publication is to analyse and illuminate the content of knowledge management as a concept that has been much debated in the fields of economy, business and leadership for quite an extensive period. Our second intention is to describe the processes carried out in developing and implementing knowledge management within the Parliament.

The intention of these descriptions is to provide a consolidated view of prevailing work cultures in general, and of democracy in particular. We believe that our publication will make readers think and reflect, hopefully resulting in new discoveries and changes in personal action.

Our original assignment was to produce a technology assessment report for parliamentary purposes focusing on the impacts of the latest developments of knowledge management on work culture.

We kept our minds open, and our project resulted in a process that was much more versatile, more interesting and more productive than any of us could have expected. To put it in more precise terms, our work led to several mutually supportive reform processes that can change our personal activities and work culture, and those of other people.

In our capacity as the Steering Group we organised several workshops in Finland with outside experts and made a two week study visit to the U.S. visiting among others MIT, Harvard, Stanford and Berkley, as well as several research centres, top ICT companies and many other organisations located close to these top-level universities. We sketched and processed the issue together as a team on countless occasions and discovered new insights. This personal commitment to the importance of effective knowledge management led us to take an active involvement in the development of knowledge management within our Parliament, as well.

Effective knowledge management on the organisational level is fuelled by strong personal input and commitment geared towards developing individual as well as collaborative work processes. Excellent results will be achieved through customising support services to individual needs with simultaneous development and exploitation of mass production processes. One pillar for this work on the parliamentary level is the definition of personal missions and core interest areas. The following four mission statements, which resulted from our work, can serve as an example of the variety of emphasis in people's interest in various issues. Naturally, these differences will cause considerable differences in the content of information each MP requires:

- Anne Huotari MP: "An equal well-being society of and by caring, participating people."
- Susanna Huovinen MP: "A multicultural Finland that offers equal educational opportunities to its citizens, cares for the weak, and fights globally for environment protection and democratic development."
- Kyösti Karjula MP: "A networked Finland that pursues unprejudiced co-operation to produce the world's most valuable competence in view of human life, nature and social integrity."
- Markku Markkula MP: "Make Finland a forerunner of knowledge society development with special emphasis on humanity and innovation."

The work method, which emerged and developed with the progress of our assignment, is well described by Osmo Kuusi, D.Phil., Expert of the Finnish National Fund for Research and Development SITRA, in his memorandum "How do we Develop Technology Assessment Activities through the Parliament of Finland?"As he points out: "In this project, joint discussions that were conducted between the Steering Group members and with various experts were particularly emphasised... This was a joint learning process that has produced many more results than any published report can express." In view of the nature of our joint activities, frequent use of the term "we" in this publication is only appropriate.

In our Parliament, Technology Assessment Project results are not only reports produced by external experts. An MP Steering Group consisting of representatives from various Parliamentary Committees participate in assessment work in a number of ways. In addition, the main achievements of each project are processed by the Committee for the Future. An example of this, and an indication of the process type and nature of knowledge management, is that we have provided this publication with an annex which contains a summary and proposals for action that were processed as a result of the technology assessment study and accepted by the Committee for the Future. Naturally, the Committee for the Future's activities are only a portion of all parliamentary activities.

In a broader sense Parliament has taken special actions in developing its own knowledge management systems and processes. The Information Systems and Knowledge Management Project (IS&KM Project) carried out in 2000-2001 was geared towards defining a joint content and reference frame for knowledge management, to create a shared vision of knowledge management in the Parliament, and to consolidate the various operative objectives for knowledge management.

Parliament's top management played an active role in chairing the IS&KM Project. Dozens of civil servants from different units participated in the teams carrying out several broad, as well as deep-going assignments. The working methods used emphasised the crossing of boarders of organisational units. This means that the project was, as such, beneficial for work culture development in several ways.

The project also assessed the available means to reach the objectives and defined solution proposals for a concrete revision programme.

The project's results have been applied in practice on a versatile basis, required investment decisions have been made and pilot functions as well as permanent ones implemented.

The Committee for the Future operates in many ways as a test unit for the new emerging knowledge management methods.

This book is a description of completed and on-going processes. It is the result of efforts made by dozens of people. Use of the English language has compelled us to view our activities from a variety of external perspectives. Riitta Suurla's skill of encouraging and supporting our team of parliamentarians to complete this assignment has been of crucial importance.

Similarly, the contribution by Olli Mustajärvi has been essential. Without his gift to perceive the entire theme within the required context, and as a concrete development task, we would never have been able to accomplish this publication. Seppo Tammiruusu deserves a great vote of thanks for his diligence, with which the difficult linguistic problems have been resolved and the translation completed.

I wish to sum up what I have learned through these projects with the following: Knowledge management is an especially difficult theme as it refers to a phenomenon where tacit knowledge plays the key role—and a phenomenon which can only be realised and used successfully with shared values as the basis. It affects politics and vice versa. Politicians must have the courage and capability, even on the highest level, to tackle the undercurrents that change our society in its entirety, by developing new mental models and systematic methods for managing value chains and processes of a networked economy. Knowledge management is a "killer app" in this respect.

Helsinki, Finland, 5th March, 2002

Markku Markkula
Member of Parliament

Table of Contents

1. Introduction 1
   1.1 The purpose of this book—main viewpoints and outlines 1
   1.2. Knowledge Management in state administration 3
   1.3. Project participants, work methods, and symbols and concepts
        for the project 5

2. Knowledge—the gateway to the future 9
   2.1 The four pillars of knowledge and education 10
   2.2 Lifelong learning at the heart of knowledge management 14
   2.3 What will the realisation of knowledge managementrequire of
        individuals? 15
   2.4 What will the realisation of knowledge management require of
        communities? 19

3. Knowledge—a multidimensional concept 29
   3.1 What is knowledge management? 29
   3.2 Various knowledge concepts: from data to wisdom 35
   3.3 Knowledge creation and surpassing one's limits 43
   3.4 Four different meeting places 52
   3.5 Knowledge assets as the core of the process 54
   3.6 Leading the knowledge creation process 56
   3.7 Regenerating activities through Nonaka's thinking 56

4. Knowledge-based activities—a challenge to individuals,
   communities and society 61
   4.1 Knowledge management from the individual's point of view 61
   4.2 Knowledge management from the community's point of view 71
   4.3 Knowledge management from the business point of view 76
   4.4 Knowledge management from a societal and regional point of view 86

5. Values and learning—building a shared reality 97
   5.1 Values 99
   5.2 Responsible knowledge worker 106
   5.3 Systematic knowledge management development 112
   5.4 Proposals to develop the Finnish Parliament's knowledge
        management activities 114

6. Applying knowledge management principles to parliamentary work 123
6.1 Parliamentary knowledge management 123
6.2 Parliament's IT development phases 127
6.3 Current state of and challenges to development work 130
6.4 Defining the KM target stage 133
6.5 MPs' Knowledge Management vision 2004 136
6.6 Development areas and projects 141

7. Summary 145

References 156

Annex: Decision by the Committee for the Future: Conclusions and proposals for action based on the TA Project chairing the network 164

Sources 167

1. Introduction

1.1 The purpose of this book—main viewpoints and outlines

The purpose of this book is to present our views of knowledge management, and to describe the various processes that we have used in our Parliament to outline and analyse the role and importance of knowledge management, its essential components and application in practice during the years 2000–2001.

In Finland, at least, a general societal view is that national parliaments should generate preconditions for efficient, innovative activities by citizens and communities, and show examples of such activities in their own work, with the overall purpose being to improve the quality of life. As a society, Finland appears to have a consensus on operating actively as an Information Society, and even a pioneer of Knowledge Society development, when compared to other nations.

Knowledge management and people's capability to learn together and create processes to increase human and social capital, are the success factors that seem to become the most crucial in competition between nations. Innovative spirit as a national culture and a sufficient degree of high-standard R&D activities will provide the basic preconditions for the desired societal development.

The initial spur for this book came from the Committee for the Future, from its obligation to assess the societal impacts of technology and the objective to improve its own work efficiency. For the book to serve as a Finnish statement in international co-operation to develop the basics of democracy, parliamentarianism and parliamentary work, it is also necessary to extensively describe the Finnish Parliament's own knowledge management processes and development steps taken in this field.

What is the reference framework of our book? The content and work methods of democratic decision-making are subjected to a variety of pressures for change on a continual basis. In decision-making, politicians must assess the effects and importance of a wide variety of factors and phenomena. This also applies to knowledge management where the basic context is extremely complex. This context and frame of reference for this book is summarised in Picture 1.

The work process and results of this book entitled "Developing and Implementing Knowledge Management in the Finnish Parliament" were influenced by the following approaches and issues:

Technology assessment and the effects of knowledge management on work cultures (TA Project), developing information systems and knowledge management for parliamentary work processes (IS&KM Project), the MPs' learning processes as a result of these projects and other simultaneous functions, plus the development of knowledge management in state administration.

These areas influence parliamentary work and are also seen in societal development, and, in many respects, even in legislative work.

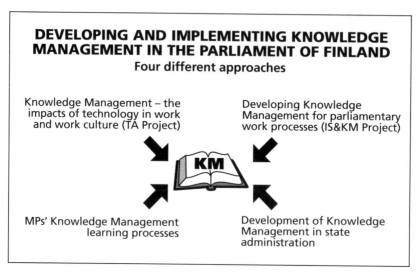

Picture 1: This book is a result of interaction of four different approaches. Knowledge management is seen as a continuous process of learning and change.

The Committee for the Future defined the TA Project objective as: "To assess the effects of knowledge management on work cultures". In addition to assessing the immediate effects of information and communication technologies (ICT), and the opportunities ICT has provided, our task was to delve into human interaction. The key issue was to learn to understand how desired results can be achieved through goal-oriented processes of change.

Even the TA Project's objectives definition focused on the fundamental issues: How does technology affect people's work methods, their need to learn, the creation of new knowledge, their ability to cope with the information overload, etc. During the projects, the MPs' learning process served both as the inspirer for KM work development in Parliament and as a mirror for what had been learned—how a busy knowledge professional adopts new knowledge management methods, ICT tools and ways of action in his or her own work.

The MPs participating in the TA Project's Steering Group also participated in the Information Systems and Knowledge Management Project that was geared towards developing parliamentary work processes. In order to achieve permanent results, development measures must be extensive, profound and focused on practical life on the level of individuals and communities. In view of this, our aim was to generate a shared frame of reference and functional vision for parliamentary knowledge management in its entirety. For the activities to change the prevailing work culture as desired, the initial stage of work must be used to define and consolidate the concepts, to define the joint objectives, and to arouse people's interest in vital matters. The IS&KM Project is presented in Chapter 6.

During both projects, we were also compelled to follow and ponder on the KM development in state administration as a whole, which influences parliamentary work and vice versa. However, we decided to include just a general description of current knowledge management developments in state administration in this book. This description is included in the introductory section 1.2.

The expert opinions heard during the TA Project led us to deal with knowledge management and learning management, in other words the measures that make the creation, distribution and dissemination of knowledge into organisational and societal success factors. In view of the principles defined by the Committee for the Future in its statements and reports, it is natural for it to emphasise human and social capital as the objective and basis for success, well-being and continuous growth. Economic growth can be increasingly explained by competence, in other words, human knowledge, skills, social structures and other preconditions of functional communities. According to the World Bank's research results, human and social capital together explain growth by a factor of four times more than that by physical investments.

We used discussions and questions to steer our work, not so much towards analysing technology or technological changes but rather towards more complex philosophical and psychological questions that call for an analysis of causes, effects and solutions. The TA Project Steering Group included a large number of their personal insights and conclusions in the project report.

The Committee for the Future accepted a summary of the TA Project, which is included as an annex to this book. The summary contains several proposals for decision-making and subsequent projects for the purpose of achieving desired societal changes.

1.2. Knowledge Management in state administration

New ideas about the state's role as a knowledge organisation are only just emerging. Within the scope of this project, we did not embark on a profound analysis of the state's knowledge management task. The characteristics of current development can be briefly described by quoting a memorandum produced by the Ministry of Finance for a knowledge management seminar arranged by the Council of State, entitled "How to increase the Council of State's management capacity in an information society" (Tiihonen, Administration Research 4/2000):

- The state has lost its previous role as the exclusive, or almost exclusive, possessor of strategic knowledge.
- The state has no right to control information or communication.
- Whether practical or theoretical, knowledge is considered to be the central factor of economic success.

- The development of information and communication technologies (global digital economy) will restrict the conventional means and methods of exerting state power (the opportunity to control information and knowledge, or control national borders, for example). The same applies to the ways of putting public authority into practice.

- The publicity and openness of information and knowledge have become the central values of a modern information society.

- With publicity and openness as the central premises for modern management and the information technological revolution making knowledge acquisition increasingly easier, the state is compelled to redefine the basis of its information and knowledge related policies.

- The ever-increasing data processing capacity has changed the nature of knowledge work. Due to its role as a promoter of economic growth, and the benefits thereof, the collection and processing of information into knowledge have become central objects of competition.

- New ICT can be used for the rapid transfer of information from place to place. The volume of transferable information is almost infinite. Information can be processed in hitherto unimaginable ways.

- Due to communication technological development, national borders have lost their significance in information transfer.

- The significance of knowledge and expertise for success—whether in terms of business profits, the citizens' well-being, or administrative productivity—is identified more distinctly than ever.

In our work, we did not analyse government decisions made on information administration, knowledge management, or associated measures taken. However, we pointed out that the Government and the Ministry of Finance, in particular, have made central political decisions that must be taken into account, even if these are excluded from our report.

In May 2000, the Finnish Government agreed on the objectives and key measures for a reform of central government. This reform policy is based on a principle decision made by the Cabinet in April 1998: "High-quality services, good administration and a responsible civil society", and on the work of an international assessment group that analysed a required reform of central government in Finland. Both publications focus on principles that are partly applicable as premises for this parliamentary Knowledge Management Project. The following is an example of such principles: "Functional administrative policy tools will help the Parliament and Cabinet steer economic and societal changes and manage the state community in accordance with the Government's objectives." From a parliamentary point of view, knowledge management is an issue that largely focuses on central tools of power exertion and the opportunities to strengthen parliamentarianism.

There is a wide variety of challenges to rise to. The citizens' main knowledge management problem is the division of labour between the various operators—the Parliament, Government, regional decision-makers, and the associated support organisations. The increasing co-operation between the various parties is a challenge to the entire nation. The development of work methods is a challenge for parliamentarianism. Nevertheless, it must be pointed out that each and everyone is also personally responsible for developing his or her own work methods, and those of the working community. Future work is everyone's responsibility.

With the advent of a rapidly developing electronic economy, the role of public administration has undergone a significant change. Regardless of the fact that this change will probably continue, we have reason to meticulously analyse some of its characteristics, even at this early stage. The state's role will emphasise the promotion of steady economic growth, the creation of adequate preconditions for business activities, and the responsibility for well-functioning administration, infrastructure and high-standard public services.

Knowledge management emphasises the principles and practices of work culture. State government has a national management task that can be summarised as knowledge management where knowledge on the basics of politics and political decisions is created, processed, manipulated and communicated. The above is a brief summary of the scope and outlines of our assignment. Within these confines we did not delve deeply into the Government's knowledge management problems or those of other public administration sectors. Instead, we endeavoured to understand the effects of knowledge management on work and work cultures on a general level.

1.3. Project participants, work methods, and symbols and concepts for the project

The Parliament's Committee for the Future nominated the following MPs from among its own members to the TA Project Steering Group: **Markku Markkula** (Chairperson; National Coalition Party), **Susanna Huovinen** (Social Democratic Party) and **Kyösti Karjula** (Centre Party), and requested candidates from other Parliamentary Committees. Consequently, through the nomination process the Steering Group was joined by the following MPs: **Anne Huotari** (Left-Wing Union; the Employment and Equality Committee), **Riitta Korhonen** (National Coalition Party; the Grand Committee), and **Irina Krohn** (Green Party; the Education and Culture Committee). Due to the fact that MPs often participate in the work of several committees, the members also provided the Steering Group with experience from the Commerce Committee and the Environment Committee, and from the Foreign Affairs Committee, the Social Affairs and Health Committee, and the Finance Committee, through deputy memberships.

Managing Director **Riitta Suurla,** from the Skills Academy Ltd acted as an external part-time project manager.

Committee Counsellor **Paula Tiihonen**, Researcher **Ulrica Gabrielsson,** Special Researcher **Osmo Kuusi** and Administrative Assistant **Minna Sevón** participated in the assessment work on behalf of the Committee for the Future and SITRA. Training Manager **Merja Karivalo** from the Helsinki University of Technology, Lifelong Learning Institute Dipoli, participated in steering the project work.

Researcher **Martin Meyer** produced a separate report titled "Good Knowledge Management Practices in the United Kingdom". Project Manager Riitta Suurla produced a number of in-depth analyses in co-operation with Chief Knowledge Officer **Pirjo Ståhle** from Sonera Oyj, Information Manager **Anja Stenius** from Helsinki Social Services Department, and Evaluation Manager **Eija Ahola** from TEKES, the National Technology Agency. The Finnish language project report included separate descriptions of these analyses as three appendices.Similarly, the Finnish language report was appended with descriptions of the following cases that the steering group analysed in its working seminars:

Young People's Information and Communication Projects, Pyhäjoki Senior Secondary School and Junior Journal;

Polytechnic ICT Strategy, Laurea Polytechnic;

Sampo of and for Information Society, Metodix (Sampo = the mythical machine mentioned in Kalevala, a wonder mill that ground food, money and whatever people need, from nothing, a perpetual motion machine);

Information Society and Values, Markkula Center for Applied Ethics at Santa Clara University;

Parliamentary Knowledge Management Objectives;

Endless Opportunities Provided by the Digital Revolution, Dr. **Yrjö Neuvo**, Executive Vice President and CTO of Nokia Mobile Phones and the Institute for Management and Technological Training POHTO;

Public Administration Development Project: Reinventing Government—REGO;

The World Bank's Support to Developing Countries in Distance Learning.

During its working seminars and interviews, the TA Project Steering Group heard more than 100 experts. About half of them were met during our two-week study-tour to the USA in August 2000.

The Parliament's Information Systems and Knowledge Management project (IS & KM Project) was carried out with special emphasis on developing the activities of the Parliamentary Office, as well as other work processes within the Parliament. The role and importance of knowledge management was consolidated during this project with regard to Parliament and parliamentary activities. Parliament's preparedness to react swiftly, as a decision-maker, to societal change, and efficient attendance to its basic duties, requires continual knowledge management development.

In an expert organisation like the Parliament, knowledge is, above all, the individuals' competence, their expertise and experience. This means that the knowledge management objectives are related to co-operation between the individuals and the organisations, and to sharing and dissemination of knowledge. Another strategic focal point is the efficient and user-oriented exploitation of knowledge.

A number of other issues, which need to be analysed in a wider development context, emerged during the project, such as managerial and leadership skills, and a work planning and counselling system. The issues highlighted during this project provide a good opportunity for the parliamentary line organisation to develop its activities.

The MPs' made significant contributions to the project's successful implementation. The Committee for the Future's KM report, in addition to the MPs' KM visions and their personal missions, which were formulated by a team during the project, are a good illustration of the service function needs and requirements for the Parliamentary Office to meet in its service provision.

The IS & KM Project Steering Group members included the Director of Legislation, **Keijo Koivukangas** as the chairperson, Administrative Director **Kari T. Ahonen,** Markku Markkula MP, and Deputy Secretary General **Jouni Vainio.**

In addition, several committee chairpersons have attended the steering group meetings: Clerk of the Parliament **Ari Apilo,** Head of Research Service **Antti Rautava,** Head of IT Office **Olli Mustajärvi** (Secretary) and Principal Consultant **Marita Hänninen** from TietoEnator Oyj.

Four teams were established: the first to concentrate on solving knowledge management problems in view of parliamentary work planning, the second focusing on internal information services, the third on mapping the needs of MPs and their assistants, and the fourth on analysing the possibilities provided by ICT. The teams worked independently but communicated with one another on various forums and reported their progress to the project steering group on a regular basis. Dozens of people have participated in teamwork and the interviews conducted during the project.

We have enhanced the readability of this report by using the following symbols:

 Extracts from the Committee for the Future's memoranda, the MPs' insights and discoveries, and the TA steering group's summaries are marked with a light bulb symbol.

 Various definitions mentioned in the report are marked with magnifying a glass symbol.

 Theoretical points of view and researchers' discoveries are marked with a pillar symbol.

 The viewpoints of experts from business life, and business-related discoveries, are marked with a moneybag symbol.

 Any issues, polemic statements and suggestions that emerged from the sphere of knowledge management are marked with the "eye of wisdom" symbol.

2. Knowledge—the gateway to the future

Two Members of Parliament—summary of a spontaneous conversation in May 2000

Member A: *Last Friday, I sent an e-mail message to all my colleagues on an important issue.*

Today is Tuesday and there are still some who have not yet read it! I think this is a clear indication of the actual state of our information society!

Member B: *How about that! My assistant is also always complaining that there are too many e-mail messages and too little time to read them. Personally, I never touch the gadget; if I did I would not have time for anything else. This mobile phone keeps me busy enough, as it is; I never have enough time to answer all the incoming calls.*

Member A: *Well, why not handle some of the business through e-mail? You know, you could attend to those matters when you are less busy, couldn't you? You also could communicate matters partly through homepages so you would not have to repeat the same thing to everyone and waist so much of your time.*

Member B: *Yes, provided that every MP had several assistants with one of them attending to electronic communication. I for one do not have time to learn how to use dozens of programs, plus the ins and outs of the Internet. I once attended a seminar that dealt with the delights of the information society. The panel chairman told us that he had searched the Internet for confirmation as to whether the hedgehog is a mammal or not. Hours later it appeared that there was no answer to be found. As I see it, one should rather stay away from such retrieval-related nuisance and waste of time.*

Member A: *Your example only proves that the Internet is a tool that requires the use of other tools, for the user to find the desired information and knowledge. To be able to manage knowledge successfully, we must learn quite a number of new things. I find it odd that people expect the information society to emerge by itself. They just wait for communication to become easier and never want to learn new things themselves.*

Member B: *To have everybody constantly fiddling around with some device or other, is that what you want? For a genuine human being, the future cannot be restricted to sitting ON LINE ALL THE TIME. What is most important is to meet other people face to face. That is real influence!*

Member A: *We need them both! In my opinion, we must find a middle way. I have personally worked on the Technology Assessment Project where we jointly pondered the types of knowledge required by the Parliament, for example. Our conclusion was that each MP must have a personal knowledge toolbox tailored to his or her individual needs. After all, the issue is not restricted to the information and communication technologies. Primarily, people must learn how to learn, and be able to assess which tool to use for the task at hand. Here is a good example of communication failure from this week. Someone wanted to interview me on the subject of knowledge management and had sent me four identical requests through e-mail! A modest hint to knowledge management professionals: to ensure reaching the e-mail recipient, try phoning them from time to time! At the moment, I have 216 messages in my e-mail. And why? Because it is December and an MP's working days are full of committee meetings with plenary sessions in the evenings. One would hope that this could be taken into account in project management.*

Member B: *That is just a prime example of what will happen if we rely on technology alone, isn't it? It will not get the work done for us!*

Member A: *Exactly! That is precisely what it will not do. Nevertheless, it is important to learn how to use the various tools and aids; this is not a take it or leave it choice. I do think that, even in our capacity as MPs, we must learn something new in the field of communication technology—it is just the way of the world today. Everyone must learn new things!*

Member B: *That is what we do every day. But does it always have to be something technical? What matters is information and knowledge, isn't it? I have the feeling that we have gone too far in terms of technology.*

Member A: *And we will go even further on a daily basis. You cannot resolve the issue by sweeping it under the carpet. The future is here already! If we fail to develop knowledge management in our own work, including its technological aspects, what will happen to Finland as an information society laboratory?*

Member B: *I know what will happen! A burnout for the entire national work force!*

Member A: *Well, you are probably right, provided that we cannot learn new things!*

Member B: *By the way, what was that e-mail message of yours about?*

Member A: *Let's go, I will show you how some of these new mechanisms of our e-mail system function!*

Member B: *No kidding, would you really be bothered to teach me…*

2.1 The four pillars of knowledge and education

 In future, learning will be built on four pillars of knowledge and education. This is suggested by a UNESCO report (1996) titled Learning: The Treasure Within. The report refers to four essential dimensions of learning that can also be seen as central elements of occupational expertise and civic skills.

Firstly, everyone must **learn to know.** This means internalising a sufficient elementary knowledge base, learning to learn, and an ability to specialise. In future, an expert will have an extensive knowledge base combining mathematics, science and technology, humanistic studies, economics and social sciences. Future experts will also be excellent generalists.

Secondly, a future citizen must **learn to do.** People must have the ability to apply their learning achievements creatively to their own action environment. Learning must not only remain theoretical; people must learn how to convert knowledge into products.

Thirdly, people must **learn to live together.** An ability to do things together with different people in all spheres of life also requires learning together and profound tolerance.

This dimension of learning is a must in a network-based working life environment. Social skills will become increasingly highlighted in future. People must be able to communicate their personal expertise to others, their co-workers and partners with different expertise profiles. The ability to communicate using various ICT tools, and face to face in human relations, is the key to efficient teamwork. It also provides the organisation with a new strength to learn.

Fourthly, people must **learn to be.** The quality of being is based on man's ability to develop himself as a holistic personality and as a responsible individual, with lifelong learning constituting part of his human existence, without continuous compulsions or threats. Sound self-esteem is based on personal skills and expertise, and experiencing one's own worthiness and acceptance and appreciation by other people. To preserve one's sound self-esteem, one must build it up on a daily basis.

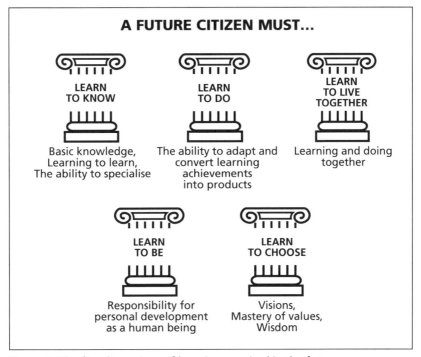

Picture 2: The five dimensions of learning required in the future.

Jussi T. Koski, Professor from Helsinki University , compares the idea of learning to be to the future wish of various organisations and working life by **Charles Handy**[1], that an increasing number of people would stop working increasingly earlier in life in order to become what they really are. This means that the transparency of values is essential.

Professor Koski thus complements the UNESCO report list by introducing an additional learning dimension that is connected to those above and is highlighted as part of personal, skilful competence. It is **learning to choose.** Choosing presupposes mastery of values, without which people may lose their ability to act. Mastery of values is the individual's capability to prioritise matters based on personal life experience and his or her capacity to learn.[2] Personal, skilful competence consists of developing the five dimensions of learning in a stable, harmonious fashion.

Knowledge provides the strength for innovations

In Finnish society, people increasingly spend their time on continuous information processing on a daily basis. Letters, phones, mobile phones, e-mail and fax messages, photo copies, various newspapers and journals, books, audio cassettes, videos, CD-ROMs, memoranda, adverts, notes, catalogues, databases, TV programmes—these all combine into an exhausting deluge of information, which, at its worst, will nip creative thinking in the bud. Professor Jussi T. Koski calls this type of information-related stress, which causes burnout and nausea, information colic. As information enslaves people at work, their job satisfaction decreases with deteriorating results. According to several research reports and statistics, this threat is no longer imaginary but a reality in current society.

> Information is slavery to other people's thoughts. Knowledge is freedom and the power to think on one's own.
>
> **D.D. Hade**

On the other hand, if knowledge provides freedom and the power to think on one's own, then new technologies will bring huge volumes of knowledge to our fingertips to entice and inspire our own creative thinking. Knowledge management is an art. In addition to competence, it presupposes a holistic personality and independent thinking. In this context, knowledge refers to internalised knowledge that is actively understood and created by the individual in question.

The effect of information and communication technologies on working life

> Knowledge management is a process where knowledge, skills, expertise and communication are catered for, administered and steered with skill and wisdom in a goal-oriented fashion.

This means that there is a specific reason why the effects of ICT on working life have beena much-debated theme over the past few years. Knowledge management has become a central theme of discussion. We defined this complex and rather extensive theme at the initial stage of our TA project , adapting the presentation by Holma, Lappalainen and Pilkevaara[3] as follows (in addition, see Chapter 3 and 5):

Knowledge management is a process where knowledge, skills, expertise and communication are catered for, administered and steered with skill and wisdom in a goal-oriented fashion.

There are indications that the increasing use of ICT and the associated information deluge is both good and evil. Currently, people have the entire world's knowledge constantly at their fingertips, and the technology to process and manage this knowledge. However, what will be increasingly difficult in the future is to interpret and assess this knowledge. Communication between decision-makers, experts and citizens is facing new challenges.

ICT offers enormous opportunities but societal changes are not always adequately observed, for example in technological user training, the use of communication media, working hours and the associated legislation. There is a need to develop new action methods for working life.

At its best, ICT will offer excellent opportunities for success in working life and society but can lead to burnout and exclusion at its worst.

Ikujiro Nonaka, a Japanese professor specialised in knowledge management and the issues of increasing human knowledge capital, emphasises the importance of creating an

Ikujiro Nonaka emphasises the importance of creating an inspiring atmosphere developing social relationships and networking.

inspiring atmosphere, developing social relationships and networking. Innovative spirit will increase through joint activities and learning together. This also applies to responsibility throughout society. Innovation and creativity have become major development targets in all developing countries. The Committee for the Future held a seminar in the Finnish Embassy in Tokyo in April 1998. One of the speakers was Professor Akito Arima who pointed out that good education, technological knowledge and skills or even large-scale investments in science and product development will not be enough in the future, unless creativity can be extensively promoted in all human sectors.

The issues of knowledge management involve entire societies on a broad basis. This KM project analyses the effects of knowledge management from the point of view of the individual, community and society, providing examples of how the impact of the information society on expertise development activities generates new opportunities for regional development.

A Futures Report of the Finnish Government to the Parliament called "Skill and Fair Play—an Active and Responsible Finland" had "a Finland of knowledge and competence" as its core theme.[4] This report emphasised the role of developing in-depth knowledge management for the needs of individuals, communities and society as a whole. Regarding expertise, the Committee for Future's report emphasised the importance of the atmosphere, prioritisation, swift reaction, and practical deeds. Technical innovations have made Finland into a world leader in new technology. In terms of technology, the nation's innovative capacity is of the highest level on a global scale. The enormous development in information and communication technologies has and is changing the work processes that enable efficiency in working life. However, mere technical changes or upgraded production processes are not enough when striving for the coveted position of an undisputed winner. Society within which people act and live must also undergo regeneration on a continual basis. This means that there is also a need for social and political innovations and new models of action.

2.2 Lifelong learning at the heart of knowledge management

During this KM project, we analysed knowledge management from the point of view of individuals, communities, society, and regional development. It is interesting to observe that each of these aspects emphasises man and the constant expectations imposed upon him. If the individual cannot change and develop, neither can his or her community or organisation. Marked changes will not emerge on the societal level unless the individuals participate and influence their living conditions and environment with increasing effort.

Nevertheless, the communal and societal levels will continue to be realities in their own right where the individual is happy or not. We talk about collective learning and learning organisations. We also talk about globalisation and market forces that are basically not controllable by individuals. However, even in this context, the requirements are imposed on the individual while the desired changes are regarded as something originating from him or her.

Knowledge management, increasing knowledge work in the information society, and technological development will naturally impose challenges on other sectors as well. Nevertheless, the individual will clearly remain at the heart of knowledge management, due to the fact that there are no universal principles pertaining to the management of knowledge and wisdom.

There are several viewpoints to knowledge and wise knowledge management, with the solutions being individual and situation-specific. Although we need to generalise matters, to provide a basis for legislation, for example, we must remember that, at the level of comprehension and wisdom, knowledge will remain individual intellectual capital.

Wisdom to ask—permission to ask and question

Striving for wisdom is a new aspect that has emerged in the management and exploitation of knowledge. Wisdom is invariably value-based. When striving for wise action, one must also ask who will benefit from it, and from whom the solutions in question will be justified or impartial.

As such, wisdom is nothing new, but striving for it in the development of organisations, businesses, and even nations, is. Even if the ancient Greeks based their town administration on the rule of the wise, and the wise alone, wisdom was and has never been highlighted to such an extent as it is now, as a promoter of success in business and communal activities. For all that, we still lack an undisputed answer to what wise action or wisdom is. This is probably due to the fact that a universally acceptable definition of wisdom is still to be produced.

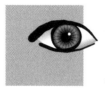

Even if we present a number of wisdom concepts by a few researchers, we are not proponents of any specific definition. As we see it, the concept of wisdom includes skilfulness, intelligence, responsibility, human interaction, learning and insight. Our wish is to emphasise wisdom as the profound philosophic foundation and value in knowledge management, and use it as a perceptive eye in various situations, examples and decisions. This "eye of wisdom" is ever present: regardless of time, place or space (see the concept of Ba by Nonaka in Chapter 3, for example).

Wisdom will remind us that knowledge management invariably involves people's well-being and their rights. When assessing the future of work, the profile of a knowledge worker, technological development, or the wisdom of a specific organisa-

> Could wisdom be divided into wisdom to learn, wisdom of insight and application, and social wisdom? What kind of working community would the various types of wisdom result in?
> **Anne Huotari, MP**

tion, the very heart of the issue will always include the individual looking at matters in relation to his or her own situation. Introducing uniqueness through the eye of wisdom will provoke us to ask and call matters into question. At its best, knowledge management thinking will teach us to ask profound questions.

2.3 What will the realisation of knowledge managementrequire of individuals?

During our project, we asked researchers, experts and one another, how knowledge and new technologies are affecting people's job descriptions, and what a knowledge worker will be like in the future, we received the following outline. Future knowledge workers will be independently thinking, responsible people. They will create their own employment and use it to create new knowledge. They are independent lifelong learners with versatile creative capacity and initiative. They master comprehensive entities and take responsibility for them. They have an ethical view of life and a positive attitude to learning. Their occupational expertise is versatile and they can learn new lines of work on a continual basis. They are versatile users of information and communication technologies. As knowledge managers they use information and knowledge to create wisdom for their organisation and the rest of the world.

It seems obvious that lifelong learning will always be at the heart of knowledge management, as Osmo Kuusi pointed out in the final stage of this project. To sum up, is it a fact that knowledge management has not brought much that is new to our work culture in this respect? Lifelong learning has been a theme of discussion for a long time. In Finland, the Government convened a committee to define a national lifelong learning strategy in 1996–97. Why does discussion still dwell on this subject? Much has been done, but a lot is still to be done.

Lifelong learners will always be at the heart of knowledge management.

Osmo Kuusi, PhD, SITRA

All the experts interviewed during this project, and the participants in various seminars, mentioned the learning individual as the most important factor in the field of knowledge management. The concept of human orientation has become almost as popular as customer orientation used to be. It has also been hit hard by inflation, to such a degree that many people mentally skip over the concepts of lifelong learning and the learning individual as clichés. Nevertheless, it would be irresponsible to ignore this issue which so many experts talk about. Generally speaking, the main observation is that lifelong learning has not been realised to a sufficient degree in practice. This is true, regardless of the fact that major investments have been employed in learning at work, or in training, at least.

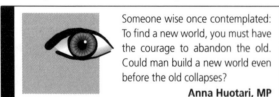

Someone wise once contemplated: To find a new world, you must have the courage to abandon the old. Could man build a new world even before the old collapses?

Anna Huotari, MP

The following is a summary of issues that have emerged as the focus of this KM project reflecting the expectations held by communities, organisations, businesses and regional centres regarding their own development and that of the individual:

1. The employees must be lifelong learners. This is the precondition for meeting the challenge and change brought about by the information society in working life.

2. A creative working community will consist of lifelong learners.

3. Knowledge management presupposes an open atmosphere of trust that can only be created through the individuals' personal responsibility for the entity in question. To be capable of this, each individual must become a lifelong learner in practice.

4. Collective learning and innovative spirit will become reality through joint learning to learn. Learning together can only succeed if each in-

dividual takes personal responsibility for his or her own learning. Here, joint responsibility will lead to failure.

5. Wisdom is produced by thinking, ethical, responsible people, machines will never have this ability.

6. We will go blind without values. The values of a working community will be practical only if the members are committed to them.

7. Tacit knowledge is in the possession of experts. Unless people learn how to share it, organisations will fail to create new knowledge with adequate speed in the current competition situation.

8. Ageing employees and their experience are not adequately appreciated, even though the employer cannot afford to lose these valuable work force resources. This appreciation derives from the individuals themselves.

9. Each individual must learn entrepreneurship at work and develop his or her personal risk tolerance.

10. New remedies are required for burnout, preventative measures, above all. Coping with the information deluge with an increasing lack of time calls for personal care for one's fellow man, plus developing one's own knowledge management skills.

For the individuals to meet the above, and several other challenges, to a satisfactory degree, at least, the communities and society must create opportunities to benefit from those factors that promote lifelong learning. On the other hand, each individual must participate in the creation of a culture of incentives and encouragement where everybody understands mutual help as a natural part of human care for others.

Implementing change through small steps and profound insight

Not everyone is in a position to move forwards in leaps and bounds. We cannot speak of success if well-being is not achieved by all citizens. The power of lifelong learning is

> Trust is required for people to share and disseminate knowledge to one another. Ethics is also important—what will people use knowledge for? In addition, values must be seen in relation to the entity in question: people must practise what they preach!
> **John Lorriman, Consultant, Knowledge Associates Ltd.**

based on consistent values, daily work, and continual learning. This presupposes the capacity to perceive one's own learning needs and an understanding which things to learn. Extremely successful individuals cannot be the only applicable model. What we must also consider is the learning tasks and achievements of ordinary people from a lifelong perspective. Requiring results over a restricted time span indicates that the idea of lifelong learning has been misunderstood. Results cannot be measured by examinations and certificates alone. People must learn to appreciate both skills and an open learning attitude so as not to thwart learning opportunities by one-sided result requirements.

As we see it, the premises for knowledge management are values and learning. In practical work, we must emphasise the importance of mutual trust and the creation of an atmosphere of trust within the entire community. Without trust, knowledge cannot be passed on or used effectively. Sharing so that everybody can win will increase networking. Doing and learning together will enable the creation of new knowledge and learning from others.

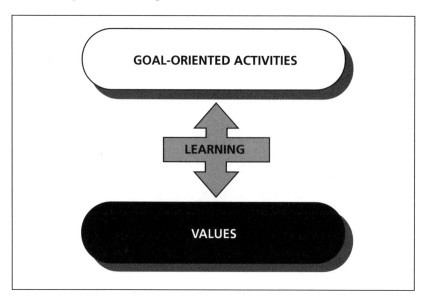

Picture 3: Basic elements of knowledge management from the individual's point of view

Knowledge management may indicate new opportunities for implementing lifelong learning, provided that we develop "a deeper insight". Supporting individual learning at the work place, putting values into practice effectively, and developing people's interaction skills will remain mere clichés unless adequate time and space is allocated for their implementation. We have endeavoured to find examples illustrating good practices, regarding the said issues in particular. Knowledge and learning are abstract, internal, human processes that people must learn to appreciate, even as opportunities, not only in terms of immediate, measurable results.

This will require trust that cannot emerge unless it is experienced mutually between individuals, and between the organisation and individuals in question. In knowledge management thinking, values are also highlighted at the practical level.

2.4 What will the realisation of knowledge management require of communities?

From the point of view of knowledge management, continuous learning and change management are among the special challenges imposed by the information society on individuals and communities. Learning should be systematic and included permanently in communal and organisational activities. As such, this is nothing new as communities and organisations have faced this challenge from time immemorial. With increasing knowledge-intensive work, the challenge of lifelong learning no longer constitutes a success factor but is the precondition for survival. This means that adequate time resources and facilities must be provided for learning.

Change is a difficult issue. It is difficult for the individuals and, at times, even more difficult for the communities and organisations. Structural systems and bureaucracy are self-preserving by nature. Therefore, change will require disassembly and unlearning

> One must see the organisation's current status and vision simultaneously.

on several levels. According to Ilkka Tuomi, the implementation of knowledge management requires a systemic change of the business in question. In practical terms, it means the creation of a common language, and adopting a knowledge management point of view on all levels of the organisation. People must see the organisation's current status and vision simultaneously.

An organisation is constantly exposed to new phenomena with new knowledge created on a continual basis. This means that people must be able to relate their expertise development activities to ongoing efforts. What exists and what is coming must be combined into a functional entity.

With regard to individuals, it is easier to observe the accumulation of new knowledge on an existing base, in accordance with the constructivist learning theory, for example. This is more difficult in an organisation where reform is more readily carried out by adopting a single new theory or model.

However, if we want to increase the wisdom of our organisation, as it is aptly expressed in knowledge management terms, we must realise that it will fail unless existing experience, wisdom and tacit knowledge can be harnessed to implement the change. To be able to manage and create knowledge in organisations, we need to understand what knowledge is, how it is used, what its management consists of, and how we could improve organisational knowledge processes (see Chapter 3).

As Ilkka Tuomi puts it, there are six basic knowledge framework dimensions to consider in an organisation, to successfully implement knowledge management. Firstly, people must know what is being talked about when the talk is about knowledge in an

> An organisation must give equal priority to change and its own vision.

organisation. The concepts must be clarified so as to be understood throughout the organisation.

"Secondly, it must be clarified as to what type of knowledge the organisation contains, what is to be developed, and what type of change new knowledge will bring about. Knowledge creation will generate change at the same time. Before new knowledge can change knowledge structures and systems of activity within an organisation, knowledge has to be accessed, understood and accepted. This calls for experiments and the launching of various pilot projects to create new practices. Change will be met with resistance as it competes with other important activities for people's time. One of the greatest challenges in knowledge management is how to prioritise change. It must have equal priority with visions, otherwise the organisation's busy people will concentrate on those activities that they consider the most important.[5]

Change requires time. Time management is an element of knowledge management. This must be observed by individuals and organisations alike. Overloading the employees with current jobs will deprive them of the time required for development. This will lead to a situation where time management development on the individual level alone will not produce the desired results. The Ba thinking introduced by Nonaka will provide the required tools for this (see Chapter 3). Learning requires times but it may be facilitated and intensified through learning together in a joint space. Creating contacts is important for successful networking.

Thirdly, people must learn how to measure knowledge, to see where they are going and what they want to accomplish. Measuring an organisation's expertise and knowledge, which are intangible assets, is a problem that people are feverishly trying to solve by various methods all over the world.

The fourth knowledge framework dimension is the formal and informal organisational structure. Knowledge management is geared towards developing methods to extract, communicate and exploit knowledge. This calls for new roles and responsibility of a new kind. Businesses have adopted the practice of nominating knowledge managers and community co-ordinators that collect and distribute knowledge, and help the community members in knowledge management and the creation of new knowledge.

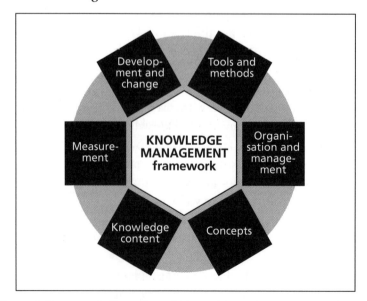

Picture 4: Framework dimensions. (Adopted from the source Tuomi, 1999)

The fifth dimension is the knowledge content. To manage content (knowledge as a product or skills of people) we need to develop expertise directories, skill management systems, knowledge maps, and other meta-models of knowledge content.

The sixth dimension of knowledge management is tools. These include various knowledge management methodologies and their representations, but also infrastructure including information and communication technology that can be used to support organisational knowledge processes and their management.[6]

The world's leading edge businesses, assessed by financial success criteria, generally react swiftly to new issues and embark on their development

> The general atmosphere in society must become more supportive of education and training with special emphasis on lifelong learning processes, keeping the level and content of expertise up-to-date through co-operation between various sectors.

with enthusiasm and energy. This means that businesses are the most likely generators of new theories, applications and models. It is also important to develop knowledge management in schools, universities, organisations and other communities. People must start learning the capabilities required for coping with the information society at pre-school and school age. The various organisations and communities must provide people with the required preparedness for ICT that is up-to-date with regard to its level and content. The universities must be able to create opportunities to develop research in the field on a continual basis. In addition, the public sector's work communities must invest in an increasingly open work culture and in co-operation with the private sector.

Leadership development

Expertise management is people management, first and foremost. In the information society, developing a new leadership culture is a must. The theme has aroused widespread interest and various methods are being developed. However, this is not only a question of retraining the leaders but one of changing entire work cultures.

Professor **Veikko Teikari** who has worked for the past ten years to develop the Laboratory of Work Psychology and Leadership of Helsinki University of Technology towards self-initiative entrepre-

> The university must regenerate itself! Science culture must become increasingly multidisciplinary and more practical. We must apply common sense, without delay!
>
> **Veikko Teikari, Professor, Helsinki University of Technology**

neurship, emphasises doing things together, teamwork, mutual trust between people, and a lean organisation.

Unless an organisation values tacit knowledge, it will not be able to survive. According to Veikko Teikari, the information society is not only a new ism or a model thought but also an entirely new era that is conducted by new principles. Free competition will pervade the closed home markets of old economic areas, even public administration. The university must also regenerate itself—not only in terms of its methods but also in relation to its culture, which must become increasingly multidisciplinary and more practical. University departments must learn how to convert knowledge into products to become more independent financially. This can only be done by working together and "applying bright ideas of human mind without delay!"

Knowledge is power. If power is not shared, the community will wither away. In the past, it was enough for the management to think and decide and for the others to do what management ordered or were understood to request. In the current situation, everyone must apply his or her wisdom as well. This calls for a type of leadership that is different from the previous type. Once a community starts developing its activities by transferring responsibility and power to the people, the key principle is trust. The people must be trusted, in parallel with their obligation to commit themselves openly to a continuous process of change.

Trust can only be created through encounters and personal experience.
Veikko Teikari, Professor, Helsinki University of Technology

How to develop trust in leadership? According to Teikari "there is only one way—doing things together—persistently concentrating on basic issues, from rather difficult to extremely serious ones, by talking things over, pursuing joint activities and sharing responsibilities. Trust can only be created through encounters and personal experience. It is a long process. It will take years to build up, but it can be totally ruined within minutes—by being deceitful. This means that building up trust is a discomforting, long-term process; however, it is the only way to succeed. If we do not believe that we can use human capital to create new avenues of competitive advantage, we should cease the current extent of education and training."[7]

Universities and polytechnics will have to find a major portion of their funding from outside the normal budget for the provision of basic education, not to speak of research provision.

According to Teikari's vision, structural reorganisation will prove to be a must within the next ten years. With the advent of a global world, university professorships will be too restricted and narrow. The practical aspects of polytechnic institutions must be verified through genuine familiarity with working life. If universities want to expand their activities in co-operation with national and international businesses, they must learn how to convert knowledge into products.

According to **Leenamaija Otala,** Professor in Helsinki University of Technology, learning management will be the challenge of the 21st century. Learning management includes change management, competence management, expertise capital management, and the creation of circumstances that support and sustain learning in a working community. Expertise capital management or knowledge management will provide the answers to the following questions:

- What do we know and what is our expertise?
- How is our existing expertise / knowledge used?
- How do we create new knowledge / expertise?

According to Otala, the exploitation of expertise and knowledge can be enhanced by creating practices that emphasise learning. The following are among such practices

- Analysing one's own actions, mistakes, failures and successes, and sharing the learning with other people
- Use of competence and expert databases as a routine of decision making
- Check out phases included in process descriptions
- Reporting learning results from completed projects in a databank
- Use of in-house coaches and mentors to support learning

Various expert groups, the so-called communities of practice, are usually the first step when organisations are enhancing sharing and distributing expertise and knowledge. People sharing a problem or an interest are gathered together in order to form a development group of the shared topic. Such groups can share the knowledge and experience of the topic and together develop new solutions. The group may operate through the Internet as well.[8]

Discussion and dialogue is the central method to increase knowledge distribution, including tacit knowledge, as described by Nonaka's knowledge creation process, for example (see Chapter 3). Contrary to conventional efficiency thinking, many knowledge-intensive businesses have created places and opportunities for interaction, enabling meetings without specific purposes. Enhancing contemporary developments in this way may

Innovativeness and, thus, success are based on the prevailing culture and attitudes in society in general. The Committee for the Future defined the human aspect in innovation as one of the key success factors for Finland. It requires, in particular, an atmosphere of encouragement and curiosity. Our target has to be to challenge all individuals and organisations to enthusiastic use of the complex human mind. The culture of working and learning together can lead to a systematic understanding of the knowledge creation processes, which are based on organisational mental models.

Markku Markkula, MP

lead to an unexpected combination of knowledge, and innovation. At the present moment, innovation is the key to success. The best innovations are not produced through a fixed engineering system. As such, even the most advanced step-by-step systems cannot provide the preconditions for optimal innovations to emerge. Innovativeness is the crucial factor. What we can do, is to arrange optimal circumstances for creativity and innovations to emerge. In addition to the circumstances, it is important that uniform terminology with connotations is defined for the matters at hand, so as to know what is or may be significant or not. Defining a common semantic content is one of the greatest challenges in managing a knowledge culture.[9]

Timo Pehrman, Planning Manager for Valio Oy (a Finnish company), mentions learning leadership as a new challenge in management training. Unless the leaders and supervisors are taught to learn how to learn, how can we expect them to know how to act in a learning organisation and as managers of people's learning?[10]

The opportunities provided by societal development must be made equally available to all people.
(The Finnish Information Society Strategy 1998)

Leadership development and sharing responsibility is a challenge to all communities and individuals. Knowledge distribution and the creation of new knowledge will be difficult unless all members of the community are willing to commit themselves to this challenge.

Knowledge-intensive work will change job descriptions and values

Knowledge-intensive work will change people's job descriptions and work roles, with knowledge management and ICT increasingly included in conventional occupations. A knowledge worker is no longer an ADP specialist but a person whose competence profile contains features traditionally associated with that of a librarian, an informatician, a researcher, a teacher, an entrepreneur, and an engineering product developer. He or she will possess in-depth expertise of a special field, will be capable of finding and adopting new knowledge, will have the capacity to communicate his or her know-how to others, and will encourage them to use their insight to grasp the issue at hand. Knowledge workers are future experts with an additional ability to analyse and assess their own and other people's learning processes. Knowledge workers are the key resource of an organisation.[11]

Development towards an information society requires that the changing industrial and occupational structure also contains a change towards service-oriented production of commodities. At the same time, the socio-economic structures inherited from agricultural and industrial societies will fade and the action models based thereon will become less relevant in society.

In 1916 it was estimated that over 60% of Finnish people worked in primary production, with little over 20% working in industry and construction and 17% in the service sector. In 1995, 8% of the Finnish work force was employed in primary production, 27% in industry and construction, and 65% in the service sector. Clearly, the long-term trend has been a transition towards increasingly service-oriented production.

Information society development has generated new occupations while certain occupations that were previously important have disappeared, with simultaneous merging of job descriptions between various trades. At the same time, the number of people employed in various occupations has changed. Some are losing their jobs while others are drifting towards the brink of exhaustion under their workload.

One of the problems brought about by information society development is the increasing pressure to process comprehensive flows of information and data. With continually increasing work-based mental stress, society must offer tangible alternatives to continuing education and versatile professional development.

Alongside abstract knowledge work, there should also be opportunities to develop concrete manual skills, innovative spirit and creativity. Ensuring people's mental well-being at the societal level is a major challenge with increasing knowledge work.

Osmo Kuusi classified information occupations into three categories based on their expertise level. In addition to these, the amount of traditional repetitive work varies. The position of the occupation in relation to knowledge creation, and the degree to which knowledge is processed, offers one basis for categorisation:

Uniform expertise or wisdom	1. Producers of new and / or uniform expertise (wisdom) who generally also communicate knowledge or wisdom
Expertise	2. Disseminators and users of expertise, abstract work (takes place in people's heads)
Information	3. Other people employed in information occupations.
Data	Repetitive work (not an information occupation)

The type of knowledge work that requires extensive expertise is continually increasing. Examples are found in the medical profession, business management, the public sector and organisational management, artistic and journalistic work, theoretically exacting teaching, research, psychologists, IT and marketing occupations, chemists, physicists, religious occupations, etc. New ways to exploit knowledge in work are emerging on a continual basis. Services are becoming more versatile and increasingly customer-oriented. This means that performance-oriented jobs will develop into knowledge work. What this will require of the employee is expertise of a new type, and development efforts of the educational organisations and the state.[12]

> The type of knowledge work that requires extensive expertise is continually increasing

Finnish people have a positive attitude towards ICT. The situation is not mirrored in other European countries. Generally speaking, the EU barometer indicates that more than 60% of the various population groups are against new technology, regardless of the fact that they were made aware of the benefits to be gained from the Internet and other technologies in their work and leisure time activities. Among the Nordic countries, over 80% of the population in Denmark had

negative or reserved attitudes towards new technologies and E-commerce. The Parliamentary Committee for the Future emphasises that values and attitudes can be influenced through various policies, to change European attitudes to become more positive in relation to new technologies. (Committee for the Future, TuVM 1/2000.)

With changing job descriptions, values will also change. New technologies enable enormous increase of knowledge work. However, one may ask whether it will only take place under technological or marketing conditions, or because knowledge work will provide innovative and challenging employment to an increasing number of people.

If people become enslaved by technology with mere commercial interests dictating the course of equipment development and service provision, the information societal wisdom vision will be nothing to speak of. When the Finnish National Fund for Research and Development (SITRA) reformed the Finnish national information society strategy, the premise was to provide a strong value base for this strategy.

Formulating a vision and strategic goals for the information society, and selecting the implementation methods, will be dependent on values. Objectives are invariably value-dependent and include—often unexpressed—choices of values. A successful strategy formulation process presupposes conscious and critical analysis of the underlying values. This calls for in-depth, extensive debate on the values in question, which may prove to be the most exacting challenge yet in information society development.

According to Kaivo-oja and Kuusi, the most significant threat may be an increasing burnout rate among the employees, which has already been detected in Finland. To a great extent, it may be due to increasing workloads, information deluge related stress, and, on the other hand, on the various requirements for increasing efficiency brought about by new technologies. These requirements reduce the need for human work and change the remaining tasks to be increasingly exacting and less human-dependent.

Meeting the pressures for change in working life often requires more than a number of sporadic development efforts. In view of this, advanced businesses and public communities are increasingly recognising the importance of developing their action methods on a continual basis, as a success factor in competition that is on an equal footing with product and production technological expertise. What is required is an overall vision and network-based development work, for working life related expertise to become more widely adopted, along with widespread application of good practice.

Endurance at work

The government launched a project titled " Well-being at work" at the beginning of 2000. This programme will be completed in 2003 and is geared towards promoting and sustaining people's working capacity and well-being in the work place. The parties responsible for the programme implementation are the Ministry of Labour, the Ministry of Social Affairs and Health, and the Ministry of Education, in co-operation with the employee and employer organisations. Entrepreneurs, agricultural producers, sports organisations and the Lutheran Church of Finland are also involved. The project manager is **Tuulikki Petäjäniemi.**

The Endurance at Work Programme has four levels of operation:
1. Distributing knowledge and good practice
2. Exploiting research results and conducting new research
3. Generating practical development projects and support funding
4. Legislative development

The programme objective is to improve the preconditions for coping with work in all stages of the individual's life span and work career in a way that enables work to be part of their personal well-being at all times. The programme is geared towards increasing individuals' possibilities of enduring in working life and therefore extends the duration of their careers. The intention is to develop those factors of the work environment, the working community, and the individual that influence people's mental and physical endurance and make work healthier, more meaningful and more self-initiated, and also make work more manageable.

Endurance at work is also a question of whether the values of the company or work place are in harmony with those of the employees. This means that these questions will involve both principles and daily issues

In the 21st century, a knowledge worker's important values will be self-realisation at work, health, safety and concern for culture, values and corporate ethics.

(Klein 2000.)

that remain constant regardless of business fluctuations: how to combine work and family life, the quality of living quarters, production ethics, etc. People who are active in working life must have faith in the future to be able to endure and find their work meaningful. Thus, the essential question is: Will it be possible to put these values, which are often so beautifully formulated and proclaimed, into practice?

The Endurance Programme has also generated a research programme led by Professor **Guy Ahonen,** Helsinki School of Economics and Business Administration, that will concentrate on monitoring personnel resources and their exploitation.

Four research sectors are participating in the project. The project is part of the government's project portfolio which is included in a development project on the businesses' personnel profit and loss accounts, financed with 0.2 million euros. Research will be conducted in co-operation with various work places. Small businesses are also participating and a separate model is to be developed for their personnel status reporting. The objective is to find the means and methods to pinpoint the essential endurance-related issues and to define the outlines for future development.

In addition to this research and operative programme on endurance at work, there are several other development programmes and projects under progress to improve endurance at work. Of special note are the National Working Life Development and Profitability Programmes, the National Ageing Programme and several projects financed by the European Social Fund (ESF). These mean, just in Finland alone, hundreds of deep-going development activities to improve people's working capacity and to create new methods and contents for basic education and professional development.

Burnout is a problem that has made itself distinctly felt in our society. In addition to insecurity and the increasing rate of change, the current deluge of information is certainly a major instigator of fatigue. Instead of a superficial cure to the problem's consequences, major resources should be directed to the elimination of its causes. In other words, we must create and implement methods that increase creativity and improve co-operation and learning together. What is essential in the application and management of knowledge is that people can process and develop their own knowledge capital in a conscious fashion and enrich the community's joint knowledge base.

TA Steering Group

3. Knowledge—
a multidimensional concept

"A fundamental observation of an information society is that knowledge and knowledge-based production will constitute its primary precondition for future success. (…) Too often knowledge is associated with technology alone. Knowledge exploitation should play a major role in political decision-making as well. Are our decisions based onfacts and knowledge-based influence assessments?" (Committee for the Future, TuVM 1/1997.)

3.1 What is knowledge management?

The English words knowledge and management have a multitude of equivalents of various degrees in the Finnish language, plus a wide variety of philosophical and conceptual connotations. The Finnish-language equivalent of knowledge may be used to refer to a single or several items of knowledge, awareness, experience and mastery of something, plus the related skills. In turn, management is referred to using the equivalents of handling and manipulation, catering for, administration, leadership, wisdom, skilfulness, prudent action, and accurate attention.[14]

When analysing the meaning of knowledge management from various viewpoints (individuals, communities, society, regional development) in relation to people's daily lives, we cannot strictly adhere to a specific set of definitions. Instead, we can only attempt to highlight those meanings which people generally associate knowledge management with in various situations: What is being referred to when talking about knowledge management, and for what purpose?

In the initial stage of our TA Project, the TA Steering Group considered the wide field of knowledge manage management and decided to make delimiting choices during the project's progress. Initially, we familiarised ourselves with the concepts in question and arranged seminars to consult experts in the field on their views on the various concepts and phenomena involved. Finding a common language was of vital importance, even in this project. Next, we worked on a mixed variety of views on knowledge management, considering the Parliament's own work, among

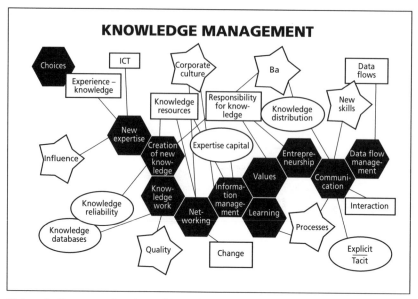

Picture 5: Conceptual variety of knowledge management.

other things, with the intention of highlighting matters that could mirror imminent work cultures and job descriptions.

During educational visits by the Steering Group to various businesses and organisations, a frequently asked question was: Is this part of knowledge management? For example, a company developing an electronic ID card did not see this as a knowledge management issue since the employees saw it as a product development project. In business activities, management refers to leadership, which means that knowledge management is mostly used in reference to controlling knowledge within an organisation. On the other hand, MPs see an electronic ID card as a product with wide implications for information society legislation, with regard to the citizens' data security, for example. In addition, the issue aroused a lively debate as to whether the ease of data and information transfer brought about by electronic ID cards is beneficial to individuals or not. This is a concrete example of the value-related aspects that are invariably involved in knowledge. Even when referring to so-called objective knowledge, knowledge will generate values, attitudes and emotions in the processing individual. These will influence the way knowledge is interpreted and understood, and, above all, how people will react to it.

This means that there are too many ways to define knowledge management and expect a consensus. The final section of this report sets out a number of WWW links with various definitions and knowledge management views. However, what is important is not how to define knowledge management but the issue as such. When talking about knowledge management, we are dealing with communication, learning, ICT, networking, etc. Depending on the context, either the technological or the human aspects are emphasised. The new role of knowledge as a success factor for nations and organisations has drawn knowledge management, among other issues, to the focal point of politics.

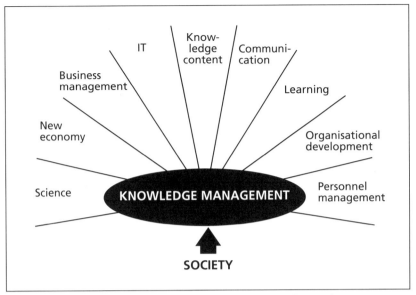

Picture 6: Knowledge management target areas (Karivalo 2000).

 The Futures report of the Finnish Government to the Parliament emphasises that a nation's competitiveness will increasingly be based on knowledge and expertise. Innovations will be the key success factor. Future expertise will be characterised by the fast regeneration of knowledge, information society development, reform of working organisations, and the diversification of people's careers and occupations throughout their individual life spans. This is a great knowledge management challenge for society and individuals alike. (Prime Minister's Office, Publication Series 1997/2.) The Steering Group decided to adopt the following knowledge management definition as the basis for this project:[15]

 Knowledge management is a process where knowledge, skills, expertise and communication are cared for, administered and steered with skill and wisdom in a goal-oriented fashion. During our project, we have analysed the challenges related to knowledge, skills, expertise and communication, and to their provision, administration and management with regard to work and work culture, individuals, communities and society. Regardless of this practical premise and our intention to understand the challenges of the information society from a human-oriented perspective, it is obvious that technological impacts are present at all times. Specific information society features, such as rapid globalisation, networking, and a deluge of information, among other things, are enabled by new technologies in particular.

Information society concept

As a concept, the information society is multifaceted, and indefinite, to a certain extent. Various researchers and experts understand information society development in different ways. Some critical researchers say that, instead of an information society, we should talk about an ICT society or a communication society.[16] This report mainly uses the concepts of an information society or an knowledge society. However, a number of other concepts are also highlighted by the views of various experts. An information society represents a new stage of development of an industrial society that can justifiably be characterised in various ways:

Information society
(Knowledge becomes the central "productive power")
Communication society or networking society
(New communication technologies unite people)
Post-industrial society
(Change of production paradigm)
Service society
(Shift of focus from production to services)
Expert society
(The role of learned people and experts becomes increasingly important)
Learning society or knowledge society
(Personal learning capacity becomes the critical skill)
Post-modern society
(Modernisation leads to pluralism and individualisation)

In an information society, knowledge plays the central role, which is clearly seen in the economy, production, working life, education and training, etc. The following ideas, for example, are typical characterisations of an information society:

- Change from goods production to an information-based economy
- Society where the economy is ruled by information and an information-related infrastructure
- An economy where information is the central product and production factor, and the overall concept referring to all economic and societal change that is brought about by new technologies
- Information age
- Information superhighway
- The age of networked intelligence (Tapscott)
- The third wave where mental strength replaces physical strength (Toffler)
- The world of symbol analysts (Reich)
- Networked global economy. [17]

Several service occupations in the information society require qualitative skills that are

> Values are the highest principles that steer all action and decision-making. (Rask et al. 1999)

extremely difficult to replace by new information and communication technologies.

As early as 1986, Dr. Osmo Kuusi referred to these skills as value expertise and human relations' expertise. The ability of knowing oneself and one's personal needs, with the ability to influence other people's values, and to get along with them, are, according to Kuusi, the skills that will help people find employment in an information society.[18] In current knowledge management thinking, these skills are of particular importance to knowledge workers and knowledge experts.

According to Professor Ilkka Niiniluoto (1988), there are three 'information society concepts to distinguish:

1) An **information and communication technological society** where computers and new electronic communication media enable the increasing processing and transfer of data and information,

2) A **skilled information society** may be used in reference to a community with an abundance of skill-related and expertise-related knowledge,

3) An **understanding society** is one characterised by enlightenment or wisdom, one where knowledge is valued as such, in addition to its instrumental value, and where knowledge management and application also involves an ethical question about the principles of good life.

From a knowledge management point of view, Niiniluoto's characterisation is an apt summary of the challenges brought about by the informa-

> Latest technologies may help people advance from passive to active learning: people will personally choose an appropriate time and tempo.
>
> **Melinda G. Gerny,**
> **The Center for Advanced Educational Services, MIT**

tion society. Even if the intention of this report is not to focus on ICT analysis, new technologies will be involved anyway when analysing the impact and challenges of knowledge management to lifelong learners and their environment.

Perspectives in knowledge management

There are several approaches to knowledge management; for example, the information technological and behavioural aspect, which, in principle, will lead to greatly deviating conventional viewpoints. What we emphasise is the human being, the working community, and goal-oriented reform of work methods and processes. This means that both of these approaches must be taken into account.

In general, the proponents of the technological approach are experts in information processing or economics. They regard information as identifiable objects that can be processed using information systems. Information technology manufacturers and software companies continually develop new methods for information processing with increasing efficiency and user-friendliness. [19]

The new means and methods of communication, e-mail and the Internet in particular, offer an opportunity to efficiently distribute messages to a multitude of people at minimal cost. Information processing, distribution and archiving are also greatly enhanced by the use of Intranets or organisations' internal networks and the various telework and distance learning environments. In place of or alongside an ICT-oriented approach, knowledge management can concentrate on organisations and people. The representatives of this trend have investigated organisational information processes (communication), organisational development (change management, intellectual assets, core competence and various business ideologies for example), organisational knowledge and expertise. [20]

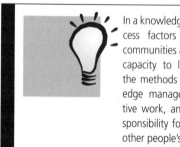

In a knowledge society, the key success factors for individuals and communities alike are their will and capacity to learn, innovativeness, the methods and tools for knowledge management, hard productive work, and the individual's responsibility for his or her own and other people's future.

Markku Markkula, MP 1999

What, then, is the new pattern or attitude that distinguishes knowledge management from the previous information and information management concepts? A central conceptual modification was brought about by a theory relating to the creation of new knowledge, which was mainly developed in Japan and contained a deeper, more extensive understanding of knowledge. Japanese authors introduced the concept of tacit knowledge, which had been suggested by Michael Polanyi, and highlighted the social nature and social role of knowledge. Knowledge is created through a social process where unique individuals and their intellectual capital are the key factors. In practical business management, the management of knowledge and expertise is becoming increasingly attractive as part of a company's basic long-term strategy. The competitiveness of an organisation is essentially influenced by the individuals' unique tacit knowledge, and its extraction for the generation of innovations.[21]

Several discussions with Professor Ikujiro Nonaka have strengthened our view that the knowledge society is one in which people must learn an increasing respect for other people and their competence. The creation of new knowledge presupposes creativity. However, creativity cannot flourish without ample space for trust and openness. There is a huge challenge in changing jobs and work places to be creativity friendly!

TA Steering Group

As such, the emphasising of intellectual capital, creativity, lifelong learning, innovation, core competence and skills is nothing new; however, the Japanese perspective has widened the scope of this type of knowledge and highlighted all the difficulties relating to its extraction. According to the Japanese view, oral and written explicit knowledge cannot express the ideas and in-depth expertise contained in tacit knowledge. What is needed instead is the multifaceted intertwining of cognitive processes in social processes. This means that knowledge management has aroused an entirely new interest in human interaction, dialogue development, networking between individuals and communities, and in real functionality of information and communication, for example in a virtual environment.

3.2 Various knowledge concepts: from data to wisdom

An ICT-oriented viewpoint is often geared towards effective data handling and information management. It generates and reprocesses knowledge with an excessively one-sided significance. Contrary to this, we want to highlight expertise, competence and skills, and their mastery from the perspective of organisational management and leadership. The Japanese perspective in knowledge management emphasises knowledge creation and knowledge generation processes within organisations. The various concepts relate differently to knowledge.

A structural analysis of the knowledge concept, with knowledge classified in accordance to its human, intellectual processing, has become widely accepted. The higher the processing level, the more human thinking, intellectual manipulation and assessment the knowledge in question contains, and the less it can be processed or produced in the form of technically detached material. This is a carefully analysed view of a path that leads to wisdom, in which technological development, however, plays a crucial role. [22]

Data refers to codes, signs and signals that do not necessarily have any significance as such. This means that data is a type of information subject matter or raw material.

Information consists of data with a meaning or an interpretation. Through learning and adoption, information can be partly changed into knowledge.

Knowledge is something to be understood and adopted. Knowledge must be well-grounded. Information will not become knowledge until the individual in question has processed it into an integral part of his or her personal knowledge structure. For the sake of clarity, this type of intuitive knowledge is often called awareness. Separating knowledge from the context will turn it into information. Knowledge is invariably a result of personal processing by one or more individuals. This makes it context-bound.

Knowledge (awareness) becomes **understanding** through experience. People associate knowledge with various explanations of why a particular issue is the way it is, and how it relates to other issues.

Wisdom refers to metacognition, which people use to create new knowledge with their previous knowledge, experience and understanding as the basis. Wisdom is also strongly associated with the quality of life and knowledge exploitation for the promotion of good causes.[23] (See picture 7.)

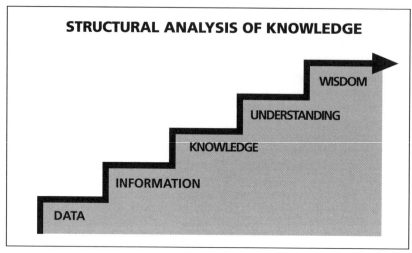

Picture 7: Knowledge hierarchy.

 In addition to factual knowledge, wisdom also includes essential epistemological and ethical elements: instead of mere knowing, wisdom includes a view of more comprehensive interdependencies between matters and phenomena, and of their significance, an awareness of knowledge acquisition methods and their reliability, plus a personally proven system of values, based on mankind's experience, the principles of good life.[24]

Kuusi[25] defines wisdom as unified expertise. Knowledge is made extremely useful by producing a single theory combining expertise from various fields. It is an entity that is more than the sum total of its parts. Another highly applicable knowledge hierarchy model starts directly from information.[26]

Level of Knowledge	Which questions does it answer
Information	Simple, fragmented knowledge that answers the questions: What? Where? How many? When?
Skill	How to carry out the task at hand?
Explanation	Why? What is behind the phenomenon? How does an issue affect other issues?
Understanding	What are the underlying motives? What is the structure like? What does the structure analyse?

Knowledge can be defined in a number of ways, depending on its value and function. In conjunction with exploiting knowledge for various purposes, its nature is understood in

> When people talk about knowledge management, they appreciate the promotion of knowledge processes, learning, knowledge creation and interaction. This means that ethical aspects, leadership, expertise and competence are also highlighted.

different ways. When knowledge is valued in its own right, for example as a retainer of common cultural inheritance, or as scientific knowledge, the focus is drawn to its permanence, truthfulness and longstanding significance. When people apply knowledge within their organisation or business to create new knowledge, for example, they emphasise the benefit to be gained from knowledge, as well as its dynamic and adaptability aspects.

Knowledge provides value and a competitive advantage that is reflected by the type of objectives knowledge is used for, and by the means and methods applied for this purpose.

Classic definition of knowledge

According to Plato (427–347 B.C.), if its truthfulness and objectivity is to be emphasised, knowledge can be defined by drawing a line between fact (Greek *episteme*) and presumption (Greek *doxa*): real knowledge consists of justified true beliefs.

Knowledge is a
a) justified
b) true
c) belief (concept, statement).

Plato also distinguishes theoretical knowledge, which is acquired through intellectual powers (Greek *theoria*), from art (Greek *tekhne*, Latin *ars*). Aristotle (384–322 B.C.), in turn, emphasised the systematic nature of scientific knowledge acquisitions and the use of correct methods (Greek *meta hodos* = along the way). Aristotle's medieval successors regarded knowing (Latin *cognitio, scientia*) as a state of mind in which the acquired knowledge is possessed as an object of contemplation (Latin *contemplatio*).[27]

A generally applicable knowledge definition is hard to find. However, philosophers seem to have consensus on the requirement that knowledge verification should be inter-subjective—based on public criteria, acceptable by any member of the community delving into the issue at hand, not on the presenter's or recipient's private intuition, subjective beliefs, wishes or preferences. Knowledge creation may be based on wild guesses or good luck but knowledge verification must be geared towards objectivity. Objectivity refers to items of knowledge that are sought using critical methods and accepted by the entire scientific community in question. In their publication on objective mass communication, Pertti Hemánus and Ilkka

> Politics needs more in-depth analysis that generates new ideas and produces intuitive knowledge. Our dialogue culture must be developed in such a direction where the justification of opinions generates learning dialogue.
>
> **Markku Markkula, MP**

Tervonen define objectivity as consisting of truthfulness and essentiality (Objektiivinen joukkotiedotus 1980). This means that knowledge would be constituted by those justified true beliefs that are important and essential. However, importance and essentiality are invariably defined by an external party, which means that knowledge cannot be objective, independent of values and circumstances.[28]

The knowledge creation process by Nonaka and Takeuchi (1995) is derived from the classic definition of knowledge. Unlike western epistemology, however, they do not emphasise the truthfulness aspect of knowledge, which they see as an absolute, static and non-human dimension of knowledge. This type of knowledge concept lacks the relative, dynamic and human dimension of knowledge.

According to Nonaka and Takeuchi, knowledge is dynamic since it is created in social interaction among individuals and organisations. Knowledge is always context-specific, dependent on time and place (Hayek 1945). Without a context, knowledge remains information. Being essentially dependent on people's deeds, knowledge is also human. The active nature of knowledge is also described by the concepts of commitment and beliefs due to the fact that they are largely involved

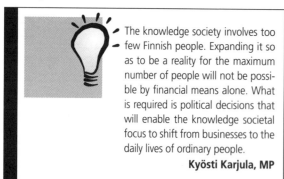

> The knowledge society involves too few Finnish people. Expanding it so as to be a reality for the maximum number of people will not be possible by financial means alone. What is required is political decisions that will enable the knowledge societal focus to shift from businesses to the daily lives of ordinary people.
>
> **Kyösti Karjula, MP**

in the value systems of individuals. In agreement with Schoenhoff, Nonaka, Toyama and Konno argue that information cannot become knowledge until the individual in question interprets it in a specific context and integrates information with his or her own beliefs and commitments.

Thus, knowledge is relational, which means that truth, goodness or beauty will always be in the eye of the beholder. As Alfred North Whitehead (1954) claims: "There are no whole truths; all truths are half-truths." This view also constitutes the premise for research by Nonaka and Takeuchi.[29]

Various types of knowledge

Knowledge can also be defined as the sum total of the information, principles and experience required to solve a problem, to make decisions, and to actively manage and carry out tasks. Therefore, knowledge can be classified as follows:[30]

- What information is required? (Knowing what)
- How to process information? (Knowing how)
- Why is information required? (Knowing why)

- Where to find the required information? (Knowing where)
- When is information required? (Knowing when)

Charles Savage has also introduced a practical classification for the purpose of providing a clear instruction to organisational management, for example, to identify the knowledge that is essential for their own work and the organisation's success.[31]

- Which are the required skills and functions? (know-how)
- Who can help me in this issue or task? (know-who)
- Structural knowledge or models (know-what)
- More profound understanding of extensive contexts (know-why)
- Awareness of time and correct timing (know-when)
- What is the best location for action? (know-where)

Knowledge is an information-based notion of the state of affairs that is determined by both individual and social factors. It is a construction of reality connected to human and social objectives, the application of which can affect the state of the ambient environment.[32]

Knowledge analysis will open new dimensions and perspectives, even in politics. In addition, people often discover new solutions and working methods through realising how knowledge is processed. This is the way to achieve the desired changes.
Markku Markkula, MP

Tacit knowledge

The concept of tacit knowledge is a result of **Michael Polanyi's** theoretical development work, which he started in the 1940s. Polanyi's fundamental idea is that genuine discovery cannot be directed by formal rules or algorithms. All knowledge is simultaneously shared, both public and personal, due to the fact that knowledge invariably involves the emotions and attitudes of the person who knows. All knowledge is based on tacit knowledge where shared and explicit knowledge is combined with the individual's unique experience. This means that knowledge is always two-dimensional: the object of knowing (knowledge) and tacit knowledge constituting the medium for processing the object (knowing). These dimensions are mutually complementary and strongly situational. Tacit knowledge frequently manifests itself in the form of subconscious rules or norms that support the other elements contained in the object of knowing.

In the knowledge creation process, tacit knowledge or hidden, experience-based invisible knowledge is highlighted alongside explicit knowledge. Human knowledge processing is a complex process involving intuitive and experience-based action, in addition to theoretical and factual knowledge. The various elements of knowledge are combined in the human mind into multidimensional knowledge storage. A great deal of human competence is based on hidden, experience-based knowledge that is highly personal and elusive, due to it being difficult to express verbally or in any other formal way.[33]

Individual ideas, intuitive views and instinctive perceptions are all included in tacit knowledge. Tacit knowledge is deeply rooted in the individual's own action and experience, his or her values and emotions. A skilful competence presupposes mastery of all these partial areas. On the one hand, it is necessary to thoroughly understand the nature of the issue at hand, and, on the other, to perceive the situation and entity that the issue is part of.

At all times, tacit knowledge is bound to its context; it cannot be fully understood if separated from this bond.

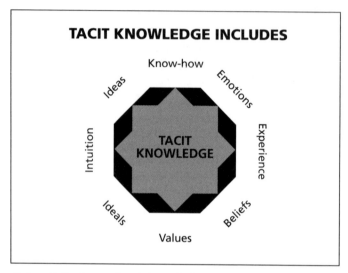

Picture 8: Features of tacit knowledge.

 According to Nonaka, tacit knowledge consists partly of: 1) technical skills or know-how that includes manual skills, experience-based expertise and skill-related views, among other things, and 2) a cognitive dimension such as mental models, beliefs, and perspectives so ingrained that we take them for granted, and therefore cannot easily articulate them. These implicit models profoundly shape how we perceive the world around us.[34]

Skills, expertise and competence

According to our initial definition, knowledge management is a process where knowledge, skills, and expertise are cared for, administered and steered with skill and wisdom in a goal-oriented fashion. This care, administration and management must be analysed with regard to individuals and the community alike. Organisations tend to manage expertise, for example by analysing the organisation's knowledge assets and developing the employees' competence. This also means that the individuals involved must have the capacity to develop their own expertise on a continual basis. Here, the concept of tacit knowledge also refers to those skills that cannot be acquired through training alone. An organisation must be capable of creating a culture that will support, strengthen and encourage individuals in versatile personal development. Cater-

> Stewart (1997) uses a skilful pianist or typist as an example. If they start analysing their finger work, they will either lose tempo or make a mess of their work.

ing for one's own competence requires the continual updating of one's personal skills and the development of new capabilities, in addition to developing one's interactive, networking and value-related skills.

Below is a brief summary of the concepts of skill, expertise and competence according to an analysis by Raivola and Vuorensyrjä (1998). According to research reports, the conscious part of a human knowledge processing system can only process a fraction of the knowledge the subconscious part is capable of.[35] Therefore, it is natural that skills and expertise contain numerous elements that are no longer (or not yet) processed through conscious thought. Tacit knowledge is continually changing and learning by nature. New experience becomes embedded in understanding through the concepts that the individual possesses and which he or she has inherited from other speakers of the language in question. Craftsman skills are typical examples of tacit knowledge. However, beliefs and perceptions of reality also constitute a given portion of social reality that is taken for granted. It is only this shared cultural context that enables communication between people.

The understanding, learning and conscious processing of tacit knowledge is mostly, and in particular, enabled by practical interaction or dialogue between people. Tacit knowledge is embedded in social reality. Partly, the will to learn tacit knowledge means submission to authority (the master). However, following the master will also enable the learning of those rules that the master is not personally aware of. To a large extent, the ways and means of possessing tacit knowledge are identical to modelling: imitation, identification and learning by doing. [36]

From a conventional perspective, the acquisition of skills has been assessed with regard to quality. This means that a skill was understood as an ability to act in accordance with predefined technical or practical rules. The success of activities could then be assessed as to whether the performance complied with the model, or whether the product in question met the requirements of a perfect specimen. In a turbulent environment, however, mere mastery of specific skills will not be enough.

Competence is the ability to apply and adapt a skill to a social environment, such as the family, an organisation, or a civic forum. Competence means applying the knowledge and skills acquired through experience to practical situations. Competence does not consist of knowledge alone, it is active and dynamic knowing that combines the knowledge content and its application. People apply knowledge and skills in social environments, teams, organisations, and their families, receiving competence-related feedback from the reference group in question.

Expertise is acquired by such competent persons who are able to apply their competence to problem solving situations in a new way. These people are capable of remodelling the existing technical, normative or social rules in the pursuit of a solution. It is impossible to transfer expertise directly from an expert to a student (through training, for example). The basis of expertise must be built through long-term education and training, practice and discovery.

Sveiby (1997) presents examples of creative discovery from the field of athletics. Dick Fosbury and his coach developed a high jump style where the jumper passes over the bar with his or her back first after approaching it at high speed.

This style helped him win a gold medal in the Mexico Olympic Games. The flop style has improved the world record by more than 10 %. Similarly, the V-style, which people initially found ridiculous, revolutionised the ski jump, and so did the skating style in cross-country skiing.

From skill to expert-level competence

In the spirit of Sveiby's (1997) analysis, Raivola and Vuorensyrjä summarise the progress from skills to expert-level competence as requiring the following constituent elements:

1) Explicit, explanatory factual knowledge that is fairly easy to encode into various forms of information for communication. Encoding means converting knowledge into information, which enables it to be stored, analysed and completed, as well as regenerated by and between users. Encoded knowledge will become standardised and commonly distributed once somebody applies it initially in practice.

2) Skills refer to practical knowledge, the mastery of procedural rules and to pointing knowledge to the material or immaterial artefact in question. For the most part, expert-level competence consists of tacit knowledge that contains beliefs, norms and ways of interpreting reality. There is no need to draw a strict border between explicit and tacit knowledge (Lundvall and Borras 1997). Scientific, technological and innovation-related codes can only be interpreted by a person who has studied how to encode and decode them. Tacit and shared knowledge are simultaneously present and supplement one another. However, it is not possible to express everything in the form of explicit knowledge. With the increasing accessibility of information, the related selection and application skills are becoming more important than ever.

3) Experience is an individual intellectual asset. Experience is the source of tacit knowledge; there is no shortcut to its acquisition. An examination certificate from a vocational school or university is but a point of departure to personal expertise development. A great deal of work and experience is required for know-how to develop into a skill, and to advance into championship.

4) A value basis and internalisation of the working community's ethical principles are essential elements of a skilful expert's competence. The

application of knowledge and skills in a social environment presupposes relating one's own values to the prevailing values in society and among clients. In their work, knowledge workers will increasingly have to consider, not only what is allowed or forbidden, but also what is actually right.

5) Membership and operating skills in social networks enables the individual to specialise and develop his or her core competence. Networks can also be understood as a tradition of a cultural community. People, citizens and workers must be capable of sharing, or at least understanding, the beliefs, norms and practices of their action culture, in order to retain their capacity for action.

The more networks an individual is a member of, the more extensive and deeper is his or her understanding of reality, and the more indispensable or difficult to replace he or she will be in interaction relationships (Raivola & Vuorensyrjä 1998).

3.3 Knowledge creation and surpassing one's limits

Led by Ikujiro Nonaka, Japanese researchers have studied how knowledge is created within an organisation. From the knowledge management perspective, knowledge creation is of special importance for a number reasons. As for individuals, knowledge creation helps them cope with the deluge of information as it forces them to think independently. Independent thinking points out the drift in matters and helps people interpret entities sensibly. Businesses and organisations can use new knowledge to establish the preconditions for innovation and for converting ideas into products. In knowledge-intensive work, such as politics, for example, continuous assessment, questioning and positive criticism are also highly important elements.

Knowledge creation is a continuous process through which one transcends the boundary of the old self into a new self by acquiring a new context, a new view of the world, and new knowledge. In accordance with Prigogine (1980), Nonaka, Toyama and Konno[37] call this process a journey "from being to becoming". Jaspers puts it like this: "Being human is becoming human." Both ideas are deeply involved in change and regeneration. One also transcends the boundary between self and other people, as knowledge is created through the interactions among individuals or between individuals and their environment (see Chapter 5). In knowledge creation, micro and macro interact with each other, and changes occur at both the micro and the macro level: an individual (micro) influences and is influenced by the environment (macro) with which he or she interacts.

For the lifelong learner, influence and being influenced are the preconditions for learning, of which the latter is normally more difficult. Regeneration and surpassing one's limits, becoming human, is one of life's greatest challenges for man due to his capacity for knowing.

From a knowledge management perspective, this type of interacting learning and regeneration relationship is a must for people to be able to receive the wealth of knowledge they are involved with in their work. Among other things, our project concentrated on analysing the parliamentary work and the deluge of information encountered by MPs. Mere adoption of matters will quickly lead to fatigue. However, if the individual in question is actively involved in knowledge creation, with the opportunity of personal influence, he or she will create new knowledge and regenerate himself or herself with a sustaining endurance.

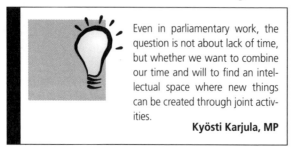

> Even in parliamentary work, the question is not about lack of time, but whether we want to combine our time and will to find an intellectual space where new things can be created through joint activities.
>
> **Kyösti Karjula, MP**

Nonaka, Toyama and Konno[38] have proposed a model describing an organisation's knowledge creation consisting of three elements: (1) the SECI process, the process of knowledge creation through conversion between tacit and explicit knowledge; (2) Ba, the shared context for knowledge creation that combines physical and intellectual space creating favourable conditions for knowledge creation; and (3) knowledge assets, the inputs, outputs and moderators of the knowledge-creating process. These three elements have to interact with each other to form the knowledge spiral that creates knowledge.

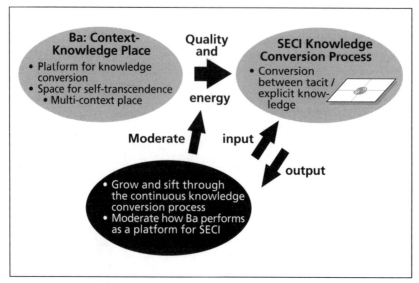

Picture 9: Three elements of the knowledge creating process (Nonaka & Konno 2000).

Knowledge conversion process

Nonaka and Takeuchi[39] proposed a theory based on four modes of knowledge creation: (1) **socialisation** (from tacit knowledge to tacit knowledge); (2) **externalisation** (from tacit knowledge to explicit knowledge; (3) **combination** (from explicit knowledge to explicit knowledge); and (4) **internalisation** (from explicit knowledge to tacit knowledge). Joining explicit and tacit knowledge together manifests itself as the above four modes that can be presented as the SECI knowledge conversion process model. Each of the four modes can also be analysed as a process.

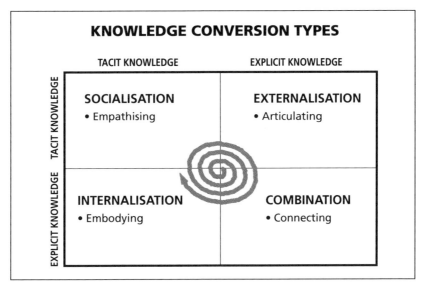

Picture 10: Knowledge conversion process (Adapted from the source Nonaka & Takeuchi 1995).

Sharing tacit knowledge (Socialisation)

Socialisation is the process of converting tacit knowledge tacit so it can be shared by more people than the one individual who knows. The individuals involved share tacit knowledge between themselves. They exchange experience, learn from one another by observing others at work, for example, and by being and working together. Without shared experience, there is no mutual understanding. Tacit knowledge includes various action models, ways of thinking, action cultures, norms, values and world views. Philosopher **Nishida** talks about pure experience that is associated with the Zen Buddhist idea of discovery learning through living.

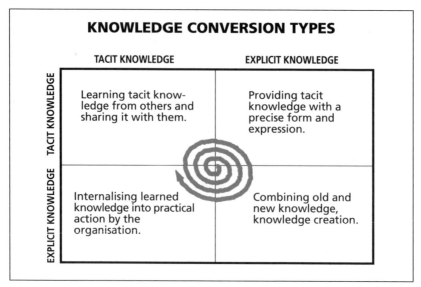

Picture 11: Converting tacit knowledge into practical action (Adapted from source Nonaka & Takeuchi 1995).

Tacit knowledge is acquired through being and working together in an environment, spending time together. Socialisation typically occurs in a traditional apprenticeship, where apprentices learn through working with the master. This means that tacit knowledge is disseminated more effectively through being together than by using any printed manual or oral message.

Spending long periods of time together will teach people to profoundly understand new ways of thinking, action cultures, attitudes, values and emotions.

Converting tacit knowledge into explicit knowledge (Externalisation)

For an organisation to exploit tacit knowledge on a broad basis, it must be externalised for use by others. This means the modelling of knowledge that is still in a pre-explicit form. As for the individuals involved, this will require a new way of thinking, in addition to good co-operation. One must be capable of analysing one's own actions and thought so as to be able to express it verbally, conceptually, symbolically (metaphors, analogies, etc.) and/or visually by oneself or by other people.

Practical externalisation of tacit knowledge is based on two key issues. Firstly, tacit knowledge must be articulated. For this purpose, people must develop and apply methods to express tacit knowledge. For example, dialogue, in which other people are listened to and heard when considering the advantage to all parties, is a strong promoter of the externalisation process. Tacit knowledge is actually a competitive advantage of the individual. It is the true internalised occupational self of the person in question—his or her in-depth skill and competence. Sharing it with other competent people in the field will enable all parties to learn new things.

Secondly, it is essential in the externalisation process to learn how to convert the clients' or other experts' tacit knowledge into an understandable form. This can be done by dividing the entity in smaller constituents, or vice versa, by perceiving the partial entities as a whole, or through creative deduction. A decisive element in the SECI process comprises translating the unique personal knowledge, as well as special occupational knowledge, into an easily understandable verbal form.

Systematic combining of explicit knowledge (Combination)

Combination is the process of converting explicit knowledge into new sets of explicit knowledge. For example, a non-standard way of combining, categorising and arranging knowledge items may lead to new explicit knowledge. The key issue is communication and systematisation of knowledge.

In practice, this is done using three mutually supportive methods. Firstly, it is essential to adopt new explicit knowledge and combine it with existing knowledge. For this purpose, explicit knowledge is collected from inside or outside the organisation and then combined, edited and processed to form new knowledge. Secondly, the resulting new explicit knowledge is then disseminated among the members of the organisation through presentations and meetings.

Thirdly, this knowledge is assessed and processed in planning and reporting to enable the organisation to exploit it successfully in future.

Internalising new knowledge as tacit knowledge by the organisation (Internalisation)

Internalisation of new knowledge is the process where explicit knowledge is converted into tacit knowledge throughout the organisation. A precondition for this is that the individuals involved experience the new knowledge significantly enough for it to constitute part of the company's sustainable know-how. This means that the individual must again surpass their own accustomed limits and find a new dimension in their own selves. Learning by doing, training and specific exercises will help people acquire knowledge and grasp it to a degree that will convert it into a joint knowledge asset.

Internalisation is a central knowledge conversion process, for example in the benchmarking process, where a good work practice used by one team is to be adopted for use by other teams and the organisation and/or other organisations.

In practice, there are two preconditions for internalisation. Firstly, explicit knowledge must manifest itself in practical action. The internalisation process will help people implement new concepts and methods within the organisation's strategy, innovation process and regeneration. The personnel are to be trained to perceive the organisation as an entity in which an individual is an integral part. Secondly, simulation and practice is to be used to support this phase of internalisation. The use of virtual learning environments and action networks is a good way of supporting the learning and adoption of new concepts and methods.

SECI describes a dynamic process where explicit and tacit knowledge is converted and transferred between people. This process will help people exploit their own and other people's tacit knowledge, which is somehow embedded in people and their co-operation. The model can also be used to analyse which values and attitudes people should personally develop to enable a well-functioning SECI process.

Sharing tacit knowledge in the first phase (socialisation) presupposes that one becomes interested in other people's competence and is motivated to develop oneself with others as well. The individual in question must see that his or her own way of action is probably not the only correct one. A humble attitude is required to be able to learn from others.

In the second phase (externalisation) one must be motivated to describe one's view to others and be interested in how they see it. This is influence and being influenced—giving and taking. Visualising the various views (a jointly drafted diagram, for example) is an excellent means, albeit a strange and confusing one to many experts. When successful, it normally leads to a new discovery.

In the third phase (combination) it is necessary to see, with regard to individuals, how the new explicit knowledge resulting from co-operation can benefit one's personal innovative spirit as well as that of the team and even the entire organisation, the growth of its knowledge assets, and the development of new products. This requires individual and joint responsibility.

This is the way of action of competent people and experts with a sound professional pride and appropriate values.

In the fourth phase (internalisation), new knowledge is exploited, disseminated and seen as an essential organisational resource to an increasing degree. This presupposes commitment to the organisation. A competent person wants work in a community where everyone's work is of a high standard.

As the number of spiral cycles (phases 1–4) increases, the issues become more profound, people become more perceptive of tacit knowledge and more sensitive to sharing it, doing together becomes learning together, innovations emerge, with increasing commitment.

Learning tacit knowledge through working together

The creation of new knowledge invariably starts from the individual. For example, an ingenious scientist may have a new insight into an issue that will result in a patent. The process is launched by the individual expressing an idea that can be exploited by the organisation. Experienced salesmen, for example, continually disseminate their views and ideas as to how a specific function could be improved. The central issue in knowledge creation is how to extract and exploit individual knowledge and expertise. This is in progress on all levels of an organisation at all times. Nonaka's example of tacit knowledge transfer[40] puts the SECI process in a nutshell.

In 1985, product developers at the Osaka-based Matsushita Electric Company were busy developing a new home bread-making machine. Their problem was to make the machine bake properly. Bread burned on the surface but remained raw inside. The product developers exhaustively analysed the problem. They even compared X rays of dough kneaded by the machine and dough kneaded by professional bakers—with poor results.

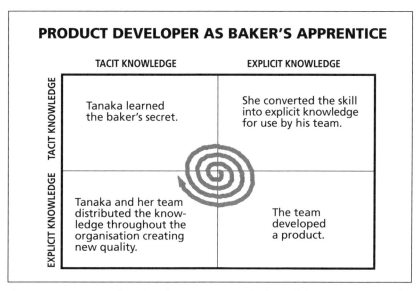

Picture 12: An example using the SECI process (Adapted form source, Nonaka 1998).

Finally, Ikuko Tanaka, software developer, proposed a creative solution. The Osaka International Hotel had a reputation of offering the best bread in Osaka. Why not use it as a model? So, Tanaka trained with the hotel's head baker to study his kneading technique and learned that the baker had a distinctive way of stretching the dough. Tanaka was also simultaneously working in co-operation with the engineers developing the bread machine and she described the observation in detail to her production development team. As a result, they succeeded in complementing the bread-making machine with the stretch effect through specific additional components. The final result was perfect bread.

Ikuko Tanaka's innovative work method describes the progress of development between two different knowledge producer types. The development resulted in explicit knowledge that could be communicated, transferred and edited so as to   accomplish a specific product component for a bread-making machine. Nevertheless, everything was based on Tanaka's experimental knowledge that she acquired as the hotel's baker's apprentice.

Lesson: Bread must be as good as that made by a professional baker. This lesson was disseminated throughout the organisation and the organisation's other departments also embarked on developing quality.

Love, care and trust

Nonaka talks about the LCT method. It stands for: Love, Care and Trust!

According to Nonaka, the creation of new knowledge involves ideals, as much as ideas. People have to develop joint values and practise them passionately. People must foster love, care and trust amongst themselves, as these are the qualities that provide the basis for knowledge creation within an organisation. The sharing of tacit knowledge, in particular, presupposes a strong atmosphere of love, care, trust, positive thinking, an unselfish corporate culture, and intensive commitment.[41]

The creation of new knowledge involves ideals, as much as ideas.
Ikujiro Nonaka, Professor,
Hitotsubashi University
Graduate School of International
Corporate Strategy

People must be given a mission and ample space to reflect on new knowledge since knowledge arouses emotions and emotions will change the nature of knowledge. This means that knowledge cannot be the same for all people. This is the reason why successful co-operation requires values, appreciation and personal experience. One must be present, talk to people, share experiences, meet different people from various situations and places; in addition, one must have respect for other people's competence and expertise on all levels.

Shared context in motion for knowledge creation

Knowledge creation calls for Ba, which is the context shared by those who interact with each other. Nonaka describes Ba as a concept with several dimensions and uses context as an associated term. Ba is a Japanese word for a place that is not only a physical space but also a specific time and space.

The intention with Ba is that knowledge is never absolute, objective or free from the context. Instead, the knowledge creation process is always bound to some type of connection. Knowledge is created in a context, it is a local process. Another possible word to describe Ba is connection. Being present in a place is not enough; what is required is to produce an interactive connection between people, and between people and their environment. Nonaka emphasises place as a term, even with regard to virtual interaction between people. In the discussions held with Nonaka,[42] an additional term, event, emerged. Ba is a place with several events in progress during interaction between people, including the generation of new knowledge.

Originally, the Ba concept was proposed by Japanese philosopher Kitaro Nishida (1921, 1970) and was subsequently developed by Shimizu (1995, 1999). Nonaka, Toyama and Konno define Ba as follows:

Ba is "a shared context in which knowledge is shared, created and utilised. In knowledge creation, generation and regeneration, Ba is the key, as Ba provides the energy, quality and place to perform the individual conversion and to move along the knowledge spiral."

In knowledge creation, one cannot be free from context. To be able to interpret knowledge and create meaning, people need social, cultural and historical contexts. Ba is a place where information is interpreted to become knowledge. (Nonaka & Toyoma & Konno 2000.)

The key word in understanding Ba is interaction. Some researchers consider knowledge creation to be, primarily, an individual activity, or learning being something that takes place inside individual human heads. Nonaka, Toyama and Konno argue that such a view is based on a view of knowledge and human being as static and inhuman. Knowledge creation is a dynamic process that transcends boundaries. Knowledge is created through the interactions amongst people or between people and their environment, rather than by an individual operating alone.

Ba is also a mental or virtual environment providing the opportunity for connection, even if the people involved are not present simultaneously in a specific physical location. This quality of Ba is of special inter-

Conventional interaction, which is taking turns in action, is simply not enough for us. We have to create the preconditions for working and learning together. This is our Ba.
TA Steering Group

est. An e-mail connection may generate Ba but mere e-mail as such is not Ba. Virtual Ba is generated when people work together using an Intranet, for example, thus learning intentionally from one another and creating new knowledge.

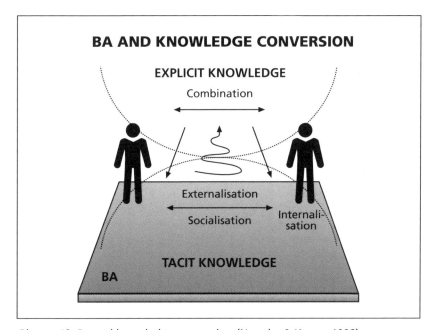

Picture 13: Ba and knowledge conversion (Nonaka & Konno 1998).

During his lecture visit to Finland in early 2000, Nonaka presented the criteria for good Ba. He emphasised that any place where people assemble is not Ba. Real Ba comes into being when people work for the creation of new knowledge in a conscious and deliberate fashion. In Ba, people must be committed, since commitment underlines the human knowledge-creating activity. Participating in Ba means that people are prepared to surpass their own restricted views in order to learn together and achieve an intuitive, experiential connection with others. Ba is used to deal with profound questions, and any participant may play the key role. Good Ba leads to improvised being together.

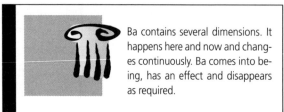

Ba contains several dimensions. It happens here and now and changes continuously. Ba comes into being, has an effect and disappears as required.

The Ba concept has been compared to communal activities, such as communities of practice, where there are certain similarities but clear differences as well. Members of a community of practice mutually share the knowledge possessed by the community whereas Ba is a location of joint knowledge creation. While experts learn through mutual co-operation, a place requires multidimensional energy to become active Ba where knowledge is created.

In a community of practice, changes may take place on a micro level, through the introduction of a new member, for example. Since communities need an identity, permanence and continuity are held in high regard. Whereas in Ba, boundaries are not so rigid—they can be quickly changed as the participants have set the boundaries themselves. Ba takes place here and now and changes continuously: it comes into being, has an effect and disappears as required. In Ba, people come and go, whereas an expert group primarily consists of permanent members. Community members belong to a community but in Ba they may be together for only as long as Ba exists.

3.4 Four different meeting places

Nonaka, Toyama and Konno[43] describe four different meeting places, or Ba types, based on two different dimensions. The interaction type determines the first dimension; interaction is either individual or communal. The second dimension is determined by the interaction method; using face-to-face contacts or virtual contacts. What is essential for success, however, is that all Ba types are required in a suitable proportion during the various stages of the process, and especially when there are several processes under progress at the same time.

Originating Ba

Originating Ba is defined by individual and face-to-face interactions. It is a place where people share tacit knowledge: their experience, feelings, emotions and mental models. Interaction is used to eliminate boundaries between people. At its best,

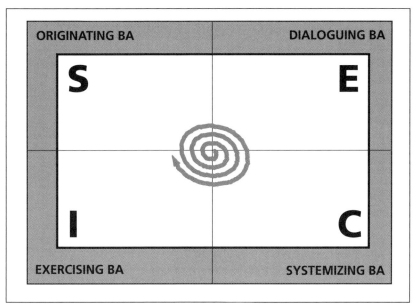

Picture 14: Four different types of Ba (Nonaka, Toyama & Konno 2000).

Ba is characterised by love, care, trust and commitment, which provide the basis for knowledge conversion among individuals. The SECI process starts from Originating Ba.

Dialoguing Ba

Dialoguing Ba is defined by collective and face-to-face interactions. Dialogue is used to promote feedback and the conscious sharing of mental models and skills between experts (peer-to-peer) as well as people's analysis of their own views. The individuals' tacit knowledge is shared and articulated through dialogues among participants. The efficiency of Ba will depend on selecting individuals with the right mix of specific knowledge and capabilities, and whether they are able to generate an atmosphere of trust where knowledge is not withheld.

Systemising Ba

Systemising Ba is defined as collective and virtual interactions where explicit knowledge is combined. ICT offers opportunities to transfer explicit knowledge to large numbers of individuals and groups of people at the same time. In organisations, for example, Intranets, telematic learning environments, databases, etc. can be used to share, process and distribute knowledge fast and effectively.

Exercising Ba

Exercising Ba is defined as individual and virtual interactions. It offers a context for people to internalise knowledge. Individuals process knowledge that they receive

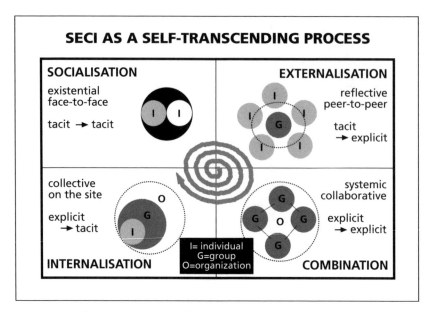

Picture 15: Different dimensions of Ba in the SECI process.

in a virtual form. They study or work on manuals, reports, or use simulation programs, for example. Exercising Ba synthesises the transcendence and reflection through action.

3.5 Knowledge assets as the core of the process

The core of the knowledge conversion process consists of knowledge assets. They are defined as a firm-specific resources that are indispensable to create values for the firm. Knowledge assets consist of inputs, outputs, and moderating factors of the knowledge-creating process. For example, mutual trust within organisational members is created as an output of the knowledge creation process, and at the same time it affects how Ba will function as a knowledge creation platform.

Even if knowledge is regarded as the central asset for business competitiveness, we still lack the required methods and tools for evaluating and managing knowledge assets.

The reason why measurement is so difficult lies in the fact that knowledge is dynamic by nature. Knowledge assets are both inputs and outputs of the knowledge creation process. This means that they will change and develop on a continual basis. To understand how knowledge assets are created, acquired and exploited, Nonaka, Toyama and Konno[44] have divided knowledge assets into four types, which they identify as follows: experiential knowledge assets, conceptual knowledge assets, systemic knowledge assets and routine knowledge assets. The following is a brief description of a company's knowledge assets with examples.

Experiential knowledge assets

Experiential knowledge assets consist of shared tacit knowledge that is built through shared hands-on experience amongst the members of the organisation, and between the members of the organisation and its customers, suppliers and affiliated firms. The expertise and skills acquired by the company's personnel are examples of experiential knowledge assets. The same applies to emotional knowledge such as care, love and trust, physical knowledge, such as facial expressions and gestures, energetic knowledge such as senses of existence, enthusiasm and tension, and rhythmic knowledge such as improvisation and entrainment. Because they are tacit, all companies have to build their own knowledge assets through their own experience.

Conceptual knowledge assets

Conceptual knowledge assets consist of explicit knowledge articulated through images, symbols and language. They are the assets based on the concepts held by customers and members of the organisation. Brand equity and design products are examples of conceptual knowledge assets. Since they have tangible forms, conceptual knowledge assets are fairly easy to grasp, though it is still difficult to know how customers perceive them.

Systemic knowledge assets

Systemic knowledge assets consist of systematised and packaged explicit knowledge, such as explicitly stated technologies, product families, manuals and documents. Legally protected intellectual properties such as licences and patents also fall into this category. Systemic knowledge assets are relatively easy to transfer, due to being the most visible knowledge asset type.

Routine knowledge assets

Routine knowledge assets consist of the tacit knowledge that is routinised and embedded in the daily actions and practices of the organisation. Know-how, corporate culture and organisational routines for carrying out day-to-day business are examples of routine knowledge assets.

Through continuous exercises, certain patterns of thinking and action are reinforced and shared among the organisation's personnel. A characteristic of routine knowledge assets is that they are practical.

These four types of knowledge assets form the basis for the knowledge creation process. To manage knowledge creation and exploitation effectively, a company must identify and map its stocks of knowledge assets. Since knowledge assets are dynamic and changeable by nature, new knowledge assets must also be created along with the existing assets as the basis.

3.6 Leading the knowledge creation process

The knowledge creation process cannot be managed in the traditional sense of management. Nonaka, Toyama and Konno pay special attention to the role of top and middle management. It is essential for supervisors working on the middle management level on various data, information and knowledge flows to meet people, participate and actively act in Ba, to be able to organise these flows. The conventional top-down leadership model is not applicable to the knowledge creation process.

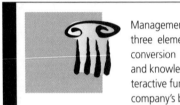

Management has to combine three elements: the knowledge conversion process, use of Ba and knowledge assets into an interactive functional entity for the company's benefit.

Management has to combine three elements, which are the knowledge conversion process, use of Ba, and knowledge assets into an interactive functional entity for the company's benefit. The company's knowledge assets are transferred and shared in Ba, where tacit knowledge is converted and processed through the spiral of knowledge using socialisation, externalisation, combination and internalisation.

Management is obliged to create and understand the company's knowledge vision and knowledge assets, to organise and effectively exploit Ba activities, and to control the knowledge spiral for the creation of new knowledge. As producers of new knowledge, the middle management will have the key role to play since supervisors will act in the dynamic heart of the knowledge creation process.

3.7 Regenerating activities through Nonaka's thinking

During its work, this TA Project embraced the Ba thinking introduced by Nonaka. For knowledge to take effect, it must be shared. With several people analysing and processing new knowledge, there is an opportunity to adopt more knowledge. Knowledge can be acquired, exchanged, distributed and disseminated through one's own network, thus creating new knowledge together. Above all, by working together, all the participants can actively learn together, here and now.

Ba is a very special place, a connection and event where people consciously strive to exploit the participants' competence, expertise and networks. We implemented this in our one-day seminars held in Oulu, Jyväskylä and Helsinki that were organised by the TA Steering Group's MPs, as well as in our educational contact visit to the U.S.A. These interesting seminars produced a number of clues on a potential future direction for knowledge management. Participation has always been an important means of influence and for being influenced. When progressing from an information society to knowledge society, it will become an increasingly important method of action. People are easily overwhelmed by the deluge of information and feel personally powerless and inadequate.

Participation promotes enthusiasm and enthusiastic people learn better. The most efficient learners are those who have a passion to learn.

Provide people with a palette of choices to manage the information deluge and chaos!
Anne Huotari, MP

The current deluge of information has both negative and positive effects. Exhaustion at work and neglecting issues due to haste are familiar phenomena, even in parliamentary work. The need to learn knowledge management through prioritisation and developing personal ICT skills is, undoubtedly, a challenge for every knowledge worker in an information society. The Committee for the Future has analysed these issues in its publication "Pain spots in the Future of Work". Ready-made answers do not exist. To be able to resolve these questions, it is also important to distinguish the positive aspects of the deluge of information. With an infinite number of possibilities, the number of options will increase accordingly. Ideas are apt to emerge, especially during controllable chaotic situations.

Ten pain spots in the future of work—scenarios for work

The on-going technological and economic transition will change working life and society. Existing jobs are disappearing or changing in character, at least. At the same time, new employment positions are emerging. Individuals and societies are encountering difficulties in adapting. On the other hand, new possibilities are opening up. What will be the future of work?

In its report "Finland and the Future of Europe" (TuVM 1/1997), the Committee for the Future identified four all-permeating factors for future success:

1) wisely influencing globalisation,
2) exploiting information and technology to the full,
3) the human aspect in innovation, and
4) governance of matters and life.

To specify its views, the Committee concentrated on assessing the nature of work and working life changes, during the autumn of 1999.

To inspire discussion, the Committee produced a dialogue memorandum and identified 10 pain spot areas for the future of work, which it considered important to analyse in view of Finland's future. The Committee does not propose ready-made solutions but presents the readers with a number of profound political decisions as subject matter to develop their views, based on which the required measures could be taken. Distinguishing the correct solutions requires versatile analysis, surveys and innovation. The Committee's wish is that exposing the issues will generate beneficial discussion to help Finnish people and Finland achieve a good future.

1. How can growth of intellectual capital and in the economy be safeguarded?

2. How can the transformation of working life in the digital economy and competence society be managed: could life-span thinking be the key to life management?

3. Who will take care of essential work for the common good if the labour shortage worsens?

4. Will transformation of working life mean that difficult and complex choices have to be made in economic and social policy?

5. Where will innovations and good new products and services meeting the needs of the knowledge economy come from and how will this happen?

6. How can enterprise be made an enticing option and the ability and will to take risks increased?

7. How can growth centres be taken care of and new jobs created in the regions?

8. How can humanity be prevented from vanishing in a hardening economic climate?

9. What will be demanded of work and work communities in the future so that people will be able to bear them?

10. How can uncertainty be reduced and marginalisation prevented?[45]

The Committee continued its work future analysis during 2000, applying the scenario methods that are used frequently in future studies. To produce the scenarios, the Committee initially assessed the current status of Finnish society by analysing a number of strengths and weaknesses pertaining to work and its future. Following this, the Committee analysed a number of positive, work-related aspects. These resulted in VISION 2015, an expression of the Committee's political will.

As a complementary description of future development, the Committee defined megatrends and a number of so-called weak signals. Then the Committee decided to analyse Finland's future possibilities in the light of three scenarios. As the scenarios' dominating factors of variation, the Committee chose the EU's future development and decided to assess Finland's future in the light of 1) a unifying EU, 2) a diversifying EU, and 3) an EU undergoing a crisis.

The final stage of this scenario work took place in early 2001 when the Committee was supposed to propose a number of short-term measures to tide over Finland during the on-going electoral period. The said immediate measures are not intended as primary reactions to the prevailing situation, like many other political decisions, but as a prediction of forthcoming circumstances and optimal preparation steps to take well in advance.

This future-related work proved to be excellent, even in regard to the development and adoption of knowledge management methods. MPs delved into the methods of future research persistently and systematically. Work focused on important political issues.

Joint views and solutions were sought beyond political boundaries, and in co-operation with the Parliament's external experts. This work indicated that co-operation between politicians and experts from various fields—encounter, learning and working together—is important and must be continued in future.

Desired changes in work cultures presuppose unprejudiced new solutions. This requires the determined development of innovation activities in co-operation with the private and public sectors on a broad multidisciplinary basis. This is the precondition for Finnish network-based co-operation from which innovations will emerge. We must launch joint projects between businesses and the public sector, politicians and experts from various fields and generate examples of good practices for people to analyse, assess and disseminate results on a broad basis.

TA Steering Group

4. Knowledge-based activities— a challenge to individuals, communities and society

4.1 Knowledge management from the individual's point of view

A frequently asked question during our project was: To what extent does knowledge management concern individuals, is this not more of an organisational issue? During our project work, we came to realise that it is the lifelong learner that is invariably in the focus of knowledge management. The knowledge processor is a human being. Moreover, the individual is also in a key position in the capacity of a handler and manager of knowledge. A personal computer is but one example of how an individual can store and exploit knowledge both at work and at home. Using the Internet, individuals have access to huge volumes of knowledge, the management and versatile exploitation of which will require forethought, consideration and specific skills. An increasing number of people will also be producers and creators of new knowledge. Regardless of the fact that the number of people having access to these ICT tools on the global scale is under 10 %, they currently apply to the majority of Finnish people. This means that they constitute a vital success factor for our nation in global competition among information societies.

In an information society, people participate in a variety of social and technological networks. Consequently, they must be capable of mastering the various manifestations of information and knowledge: linguistic,

> How can a small minority demand personal services, especially public ones that are financed by taxpayers, if the majority accepts and uses the Internet?
>
> **Paula Tiihonen, Committee Counsellor**

information technological, cultural, and pictorial communication.

People must be capable of individual and social decision-making and understand the complex interdependencies in the current societal and economic system.

In an information society, the individuals will have increasing freedom of action; at the same time, however, their own responsibility will increase accordingly with regard to their personal success in life.

In their own lives, individuals must have a variety of skills that are required for the management, wise and proficient care for knowledge, competence, expertise and communication—in addition to goal-oriented leadership.

An ideal situation: Knowledge management requires people who can think, find the essential knowledge, exploit it in their work and produce innovative solutions at the same time.
Anne Huotari, MP

While pondering on this theme, a personal profile started to emerge. After hearing experts in the field, this profile manifested itself as that of a knowledge professional, which also seems to fit the members of an information society on a more general basis. He or she is a lifelong learner who adopts a constructive, albeit a critical attitude towards his or her environment. These people have versatile skills for life management, co-operation, interaction, and communication—in addition to their technological and professional skills. They can adapt to the changes of technology, production, internationalisation, communication, and civic life. They are creative and active operators, in addition to being unique, multitalented creative individuals who can combine various factors in a free action environment and perceive their environment in new ways.[46]

"The Committee for the Future has established two discussion forums:
1) The Forum of the Experienced and Wise, and 2) The Forum of the Young Future-Builders. These forums concentrate on specific future-related issues in co-operation with the Committee, and convene in joint meetings as necessary. As the young people convened in the Parliament House in mid-June 2000, to discuss the use of the Internet, among other things, many of us realised a minor issue that can promote equality in the current situation where the entire information technological and political world is talking about the Digital Divine. However small, this issue is important in principle. When a young, hearing-impaired person from northern Finland spoke enthusiastically about his participation in various societal activities through the Internet, we realised that the Internet enabled him—perhaps for the first time in his 20 years—to feel genuinely equal to others."
Paula Tiihonen, Committee Counsellor

Knowledge is the capacity to act

Esko Kilpi, Management Consultant, perceives it as follows: If knowledge is understood as the capacity to act and develop activities, the key questions regarding the individual will be: 1) What is the capacity that the individual uses for action? and 2) How can he or she develop his or her total capacity and situation-specific capacity on a continual basis? Mere routine repetition of work tasks will not be enough in the future. Nowadays, the bulk of production, regarding services and any other products alike, is generated through customised, situation and event specific solutions in co-operation with the client. Therefore, it is crucial for the individual to have the capacity to creatively apply his or her competence, expertise and knowledge. What is also required is the capacity for knowledge creation together with other people, in addition to the knowledge acquisition capacity. The individual must have a sufficient, optimal base of knowledge, competence and expertise complying with the specific task at hand, plus the ability to act there and then. This is the current trend of change in many conventional jobs and work assignments. Clients increasingly require more knowledge and an individual service—and they are also prepared to pay for it.[47]

The profile of a knowledge professional—from obedience to responsibility

Kilpi sees the profile of a knowledge professional as follows: A knowledge professional does not repeat things. He or she does not act according to other people's instructions but uses his or her own skills, competence and expertise, and thinks independently. Knowledge and action are combined. Success in

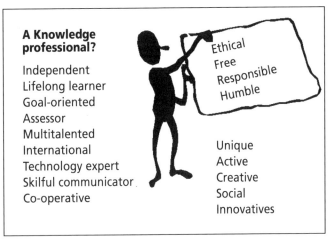

A Knowledge professional?

Independent
Lifelong learner
Goal-oriented
Assessor
Multitalented
International
Technology expert
Skilful communicator
Co-operative

Ethical
Free
Responsible
Humble

Unique
Active
Creative
Social
Innovatives

knowledge work is based on voluntary action, not on external commands since thinking requires the use of personal creativity. Regarding the prevailing work culture this means a shift from obedience to personal responsibility.

There is a relationship of responsibility between employers and employees. Therefore, a change is required regarding the idea that if the manager has the responsibility for a project, an employee has none. This view is fundamentally wrong as it is based on the child-parent relationship, not on one between two responsible adults. Knowledge workers own their thoughts and are responsible for updating their personal expertise on a continual basis. The central issue is not to develop activities but to learn how to identify the matters to be avoided, and those to be regenerated.[48]

Successful knowledge distribution and dissemination is essential in knowledge work. This is achieved through interactive discussion (dialogue) where all parties learn. Within an organisation, the vision must also be explained and shared, not only distributed electronically or by using OHP transparencies.

Human relations will become increasingly important. Knowledge and ideas must be exchanged and processed, even without an agenda. This presupposes free dialogue and an ability to identify the participants' prevailing emotional attitudes.

What does knowledge work and knowledge-intensive mean in practice?

Knowledge work is not confined to ADP work, or even the increasing use of experts. Any assignment emphasising the requirements imposed on the reception, processing and creation of new knowledge, can be defined as knowledge-intensive work.

People act based on various meanings and connotations, and create them. Direct transfer of understanding is not possible. Each individual must personally produce the interpretations—what is not understood cannot be seen. The central issue in knowledge work is to give people the opportunity and space to see for themselves and understand their personal choices. This is also the only way to personal responsibility.

All people are creative and restricted in certain respects. Understanding one's own incompleteness and uniqueness is the key to human development and co-operation in knowledge work. It is not necessary for everyone to be as proficient as others in everything, provided that we can jointly benefit from other people's skills.

At their best, knowledge professionals master the required technological skills and have the capacity for intuitive thinking.

To be able to exploit diversity through learning together, we must learn to identify difference and tolerate it in other people. Knowledge is not only transferred, it is created together.[49]

Davenport and Prusak (1998) talk about knowledge-oriented personnel, which, according to them, includes all the employees of the business in question. As they see it, everyone must create, distribute, acquire and use knowledge in their daily routines. This means that knowledge management must be an integral part of everyone's work.

Our most valuable capital is contained in our heads. It transfers with us wherever we go—without a passport, visa, machines, equipment or bags.

Riitta Korhonen, MP

The competence of a good knowledge professional includes "hard expertise" or mastery of information systems, technical skills, and professional experience, plus "soft skills", or mastery of cultural, political and personal knowledge. Multitalented teams possess a variety of cultural, political and individual dimensions. The minimum requirement is for each team member to master a specific area, with the others respecting this expertise. This will allow the entire team to exploit the competence of all members in joint activities.[50]

Individual entrepreneurship

Professor **Paula Kyrö,** a developer of entrepreneurship pedagogy, talks about individual entrepreneurship alongside entrepreneurship and intrapreneurship. Entrepreneurship conventionally refers to a small business with the entrepreneur as the owner and business manager. Intrapreneurship is used in reference to a micro-level working community or an organisational action method that resembles entrepreneurship. Individual entrepreneurship is used in reference to the individual's changing role in the post-modern transitory period where the division of labour and the idea of an organisation's action methods are changing. Individual entrepreneurship describes an individual's personal behaviour, attitudes and action methods. This may also include the idea that an employee can own a specific part of the organisation, which is not a characteristic feature, however. Rather, the idea implies the individual's personal responsibility for his or her own employment and income, plus the associated benefits and risks.

As a concept, entrepreneurship includes change. This makes it an interesting theme for the survey of challenges encountered in knowledge work, especially from the perspective of an individual. Entrepreneurship will change existing action methods, hierarchy and bureaucracy. It has human action as its central element, with the operator being, as Kyrö describes, a unique, complex, innovative, free, daring, creative and responsible person. In individual entrepreneurship, the individual exerts influence on himself or herself and his or her environment. Individual entrepreneurs are active operators and opinion leaders in their own communities. These are also the qualities that were mentioned in conjunction with the future knowledge professionals above. The challenges include responsibility and risks, with freedom and creativity as the promise. Man has always been happy being free but it may be asked whether he can rise to and stand the required responsibility that also involves larger entities—nature and humanity. [51]

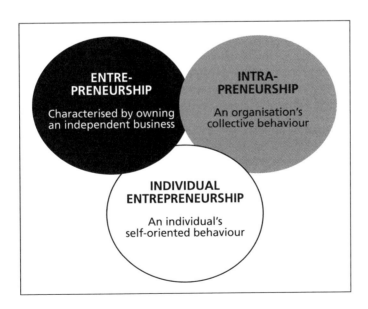

Picture 16: Different forms of entrepreneurship (Adapted from source, Kyrö 1998).

Creativity emphasises goal-oriented activities

In an information society, citizens are expected to be creative and capable of intuitive thinking, due to the fact that expertise is based on knowledge and the creation of new knowledge.

> In the US, young people no longer want safe long-term employment in large companies. An intellectual void is not attractive! What young people want is intellectual activity and being challenged as entrepreneurs!
>
> **Kari Laento, Senior Vice President, Sonera Corporation.**

When competing in terms of competence and expertise, creativity and an innovative spirit must be permanent employee qualities—not something occasional resulting from a particular inspiration. This is a major challenge to individuals, organisations, and society in its entirety.

Mihaly Csikszentmihaly (1996) has carried out research into creativity, with very interesting results regarding the profile of a knowledge professional. His research findings indicate that creativity is generated through interaction between individuals and a socio-cultural context. As a phenomenon, creativity is systemic and not restricted to individuals alone. Creativity cannot flourish without support, freedom, feedback and encouragement. Csikszentmihaly talks about an optimal experience (flow) that is enjoyable and rewarding in itself. This type of experience is typical of creative people.

The central features of a flow experience

- The objectives for action are clearly identified at all times. We always know what to do next.
- Action is followed by immediate feedback.
- There is a harmonious proportion between the challenge encountered and the skills of the individual performing the task in question.
- Action and the individual's awareness are unified.
- People exclude any disturbing factors from their awareness.
- There is no fear of failure. Fear of failure or "being wrong" prevents creativity.
- Action is autotelic—an end in itself.
- Self-awareness disappears.
- The track of time becomes blurred.

Creative people get satisfaction from working towards self-defined goals and jobs well done. They are passionate learners and optimists who listen carefully to their emotions and intuition. They are complex people whose action models include seemingly contradictory characteristics that are typical of creative individuals. They may be energetic but self-effacing, intelligent and naive, playful and disciplined, imaginative but realistic, humble and proud, traditional but revolutionary.[52]

From a systemic perspective, as Csikszentmihaly sees it, creativity consists of interaction between three elements:

- a culture that contains symbolic rules,
- people who reform the symbolic rules of this culture, and
- communities of practice who identify and approve the innovations made by creative people and thus cause the regeneration of the symbolic cultural rules.

Even here, the issue is the interaction between individuals and communities, and the tolerance of innovation and innovative people. If organisations want to retain creative people in their employment, the management must pay particular attention to matching the creative people's personal objectives to those of the organisation. If creative people do not experience current challenges and objectives as their own, or if these are difficult to identify, they will soon grow tired of the organisation.

This clearly demonstrates the voluntary nature of participation, which Kilpi emphasised. Creative people's objectives are based on voluntariness. They really want to realise their objectives. In addition, creative people are future-oriented. If they cannot see any possibilities in the would-be future, they will become frustrated.[53]

> Creativity on its own is not enough for innovation. People and communities can be creative, but new inventions, ideas and thoughts do not necessarily lead to innovations. Innovative persons or communities are able to make effective use of both their own and others' ideas and convert them into functioning innovations.
>
> (Committee for the Future, TuVM 1/ 1997.)

Limited specialisation will impede creativity in organisations and society. An example is the increasing diversification between the various fields of science and other symbolic systems. Concurrently, this will also lead to isolation and decreasing opportunities for creativity. In an information society, for example the jargon used by ITC specialist—the "technological argy-bargy", or the linguistic confusion in the interaction between scientists from various fields, is especially dangerous. According to Csikszentmihaly, one of the central mechanisms in creativity is the understanding and generation of interconnections between different types of knowledge and various symbolic fields.[54]

> One of the challenges for an expert society is to enable an open debate culture and eliminate secrecy. If debate only takes place in closed communities or businesses, there will exist the danger of losing sight and being cast adrift. The expression of different views and opinions presupposes extensive co-operation between businesses and universities, for example. This kind of openness cannot be achieved if everyone only looks after their own interest.
>
> **Osmo Kuusi, Ph.D., SITRA**

The Futures Report of the Finnish Government to the Parliament, Part II, mentions that "A nation that can construct not only an information superhighway but a creativity superhighway has a strategic edge in expertise-based competition" (Prime Minister's Office, Publication Series 1997/4).

The profile of a knowledge professional is quite similar to that of any person engaged in creative work. From the organisation's perspective, however, it must be pointed out that independent, strongly goal-oriented individuals are also demanding and not often good employees. To be able to achieve the ideal profile of a knowledge professional, at least to a sufficient degree, it must take place in a co-operative, responsible and ethically transparent action environment. Based on the views of various experts writing on the information society, we can conclude that the parties compelled to rise to this challenge include individuals, communities and society alike.

General technological education—an integral part of the information society

Regardless of the fact it has not been possible to scientifically prove whether people can be educated and trained to be creative and innovative or not, it has been observed, nevertheless, that the amount of creative and innovative activities will decrease under unfavourable circumstances. Esa-Matti Järvinen, MEd, Project Manager from the University of Oulu, (55) has carried out research into this and developed a special type of pedagogy. This can be used creatively in practice to teach

For young people to learn to how assume responsibility, they must be given responsible tasks.

Kyösti Karjula, MP

children, even at an early age, to understand what technology (Greek techne = skill and logos = knowledge) is and how to exploit it, in order to develop their inventiveness. Naturally, an additional objective is to provide young people with the ways and means to cope with the information society. The basic idea is that a man-made environment is also a significant issue and worth teaching at our schools. Technological education will help children become familiar with an environment built by man for his own needs. In addition, our technological environment has a strong social role. Children must be brought up so that they can understand, appreciate, use, assess, and continue the development of our technological environment.

In technological fields, teaching cannot be geared towards finding the correct answers. There simple are no correct answers to the questions asked.

Esa-Matti Järvinen, MEd, Project Manager, University of Oulu

Technological development and the related transfer of know-how from one generation to another is one of our basic duties, similar to that of the craftsman and artisan generations. In view of the tremendous current technological development, we must ensure optimal availability of the required technological knowledge and competence to coming generations on a comprehensive basis, without forgetting the ethical and moral questions. The school curriculum must also be up-to-date regarding the prevailing technological reality in people's daily lives. This is essential, from the perspective of general education, and the competitiveness of those industries that exploit and develop high technology.

More often than not, people take technology for granted in their lives and never stop to think about it. Therefore, it is very important to clearly indicate to children, even at a very

Mere knowing is not a skill but knowing how to use knowledge in new contexts is.

Anne Huotari, MP

early age, that they use various technological applications on a daily basis. A general aim of technological education can be to increase children's awareness, assessment and appreciation of our living environment.

To develop children's problem solving skills must be one of the key objectives in technological study. In technological fields, teaching cannot be geared towards finding the correct answers. There simply are no correct answers to the questions asked. This is a challenge to teachers, as they must develop and create new things in co-operation with children, in addition to assessing and correcting existing solutions.[56]

A challenge is also posed by the fact that children or young people are frequently much more proficient users of new technological tools than their parents and teachers. This is a situation where adults may lose their authority. For example, when a father asks his daughter for instructions on web page design. Is this a desirable development? How could these conflicts of authority be prevented in advance?

It is an odd fact that we carefully teach our children to obey the traffic regulations but never instruct them on surfing the Internet. Do we even tell them why certain pages are not intended for children? Can we really tell them why this is?

Susanna Huovinen, MP

Technological education—children must be brought up to:

- Perceive, test and use technology on a versatile basis in their lives,
- Think about the effects of technology in our lives and mankind's development,
- Appreciate technology as an element that enables our lives and makes life easier, safer and more comfortable,
- Understand the technology that surrounds us, and its central principles of operation,
- Design, produce and apply technology, as much as possible, to be able to solve problems and the needs arising from their personal life environment,
- Understand and experience connections between mathematics, the natural sciences and technology in practical life,
- Follow up technological implications both on the individual and the communal level,
- Constructively assess "ready-made" technological applications and those produced personally.

In addition, children must be brought up to:

- Accept a responsible view of technology based on jointly accepted ethical values,
- Be aware of the existing problems caused by technology in our immediate environment,
- Critically assess whether a specific technology is suitable or unsuitable, applicable or inapplicable, dangerous or safe with positive or negative side effects for a specific purpose, etc.,
- Look for remedial suggestions and solutions to technology-induced everyday problems, which they have personally encountered.[57]

Career criteria focusing on individuality and lifelong learning

According to Stewart, Raivola and Vuorensyrjä[58] the new career criteria that focus on individuality and lifelong learning can be summarised by the following questions:

- Do you still feel that you are learning? Do you know what you have learned and what remains to be learned in order to cope with the challenges at hand? Does your (work) organisation support your learning? The skill to use those learning support systems that are external to formal educational systems will become increasingly important.

- If your job were advertised as a vacancy today, could you still beat the competition for it? In other words, have you striven to maintain your competitiveness?

- Do you let others take advantage of you? Do you often sacrifice yourself to perform routine tasks at the expense of your personal growth? Do people often apply to your loyalty as the one who 'does the job' in situations where the rest of the personnel may be in training, for example? It appears obvious that an investment in you is an investment wasted.

- Can you define the exact benefit you are to your organisation, and your added value to the client? You should be aware of this value, in view of the coming result and development discussions with your superiors.

- Would you know what to do if you lost your job? In other words, are you aware of the market value of your personal expertise?

- Do you still enjoy your work? Are you exhausted and no longer see any challenges in your organisation? Are you looking forward to your retirement? On Mondays, do you wish it were already Friday?

- How many people in your community can do your job as well or better than you? If you were absent for a long time, would it have any effect on other people's working pace or on the performance of your organisation?

- Can other people learn your present job quickly? Is it easy to find a substitute for you? In other words, are you easy to replace?

- How many networks or teams are you a member of in your work community and its client contacts? Are you located at the network nodes or at the extreme branch points?

- Your career is not necessarily coming to an end, even if you have answered some questions above to your disadvantage, provided that you are indispensable to the clients' success. Consequently, breaking the symbiotic relation between you and your clients would inflict damage to all parties involved.

4.2 Knowledge management from the community's point of view

Regarding information society discussion, the theme of knowledge, expertise and learning opens a viewpoint on more effective exploitation of human resources, distribution of power and responsibility, and networking between various organisations. During the 1990s, it has become increasingly evident that the success of businesses and public organisations alike, will depend on the knowledge, competence and expertise of individual employees and independent professional teams, and their networking co-operation. People possess knowledge, competence and expertise that cannot be exploited in the same way as machines and equipment. Making a difference will be both human and economically advisable. Up-to-date, commercially valuable knowledge and expertise cannot exist without learning.

> In the public administration sector, people must be developed and trained for team work and networking. Civil servants must have networks with various interest groups and civic organisations and contacts to specialists in the field, both in business life and the public sector. No single individual can alone judge whether a specific solution is correct for Finland or not. There will be an increasing need for co-operation in the information society.
>
> **Auni-Marja Vilavaara, Legal Advisor, Deputy Director of Administration**

Raivola and Vuorensyrjä point out that if people have learned anything about the theory of learning on the whole, it can be summarised by stating that learning is not a chain of events, and cannot be understood if detached from the learner's personal appreciation and commitments. In reality, learning is fuelled by the personal needs and commitments of the individual in question. "Central expertise of an international standard is generated through long-term commitment and intensive learning. Intensive learning is learning with a passion. This passion is based on elements that are personally significant to the learners themselves."[59]

> Intensive learning is learning with a passion.

When talking about knowledge management from the community's point of view, the individual will be invariably involved in due course. Naturally, this is due to the fact that knowledge is created by people. An organisation's knowledge assets cannot increase without innovative individuals.

However, people must be provided with increasingly extensive opportunities for learning and knowledge distribution. Co-operation between the public and private sectors is a must if innovative activities are not to become the exclusive property of a few successful companies. In research and development activities, networking must refer to co-operation between businesses, universities, schools, various organisations, public administration and political parties. The Internet will enable rapid transfer of knowledge and expertise but knowledge cannot be effective without a culture of mutual sharing.

Knowing is a social phenomenon

In business competition for markets and success, a well-functioning organisation with an efficient management and decision-making personnel is considered to be the precondition for success. Nevertheless, an excellent product is not enough. A good organisation exploits the knowledge, skills and expertise of its entire personnel. Its internal management system is encouraging and focused on participation. (Committee for the Future, TuVM 1/1997.)

Knowledge management emphasises the building of an atmosphere of trust and openness. In future, leaders must base their activities on corporate values as well as their own. They must be able to help people build a work environment where knowledge can flow free of obstructions. Csikszentmihaly emphasises that, for creative people, it is important to understand the objectives of action and to be allowed to implement them without obstructions. This also means that they must be fully aware of the company's objectives, to be able to match their own objectives to them. The same also applies to values.

According to **Esko Kilpi**[60], successful communities always have a particular reason, an objective for their existence. To reach the objective, individuals must also work more efficiently

Individuals have limited capabilities, this is why they need other people.
Esko Kilpi, Management Consultant, Sedecon Consulting

together, complement one another and challenge themselves to learn together. Individuals have limited capabilities, this is why they need other people. Through the joint efforts of individuals, and the sum total of various talents and capabilities, communities endeavour to build entities that are larger than the sum of their components. This is an advantage to the community, and the precondition for the task's successful implementation; moreover, it is also an advantage to the individuals as they can surpass their personal limits with the aid of other people. At its most efficient, knowing is a social phenomenon.

In knowledge management development activities, organisations should realise that there is no single correct solution. Instead, knowledge management should be understood from the perspective of the organisation's own premises and challenges. This calls for internal analysis, prior to embarking on activities of a new type.

As Kilpi sees it, the future concept of intellectual capital will include the idea that each employee is his or her own employer and personally responsible for the development of his or her own expertise. Consequently, lifelong learning in itself will not be enough—the continual verification of lifelong learning results will become an increasingly central issue. Practical demonstration tests, for example, which are a typical feature of a young person's study, will become increasingly central in adult education as well. An individual must have a lifelong work diary, in addition to his or her lifelong learning achievements diary—a personal employment portfolio. The learning achievements diary is used to collect information and material for the individual to present his or her personal competence.

In principle, as modern technology provides access to any information and knowledge, the focus of professional expertise is not placed on the content of knowledge. Instead, it will be shifted onto search and retrieval capabilities, and those required in processing the knowledge obtained into situation-specific views and solutions. The effort to increase people's personal capacity will not only focus on increasing their personal knowledge but also on improving their ability to look for and find the required knowledge. Correspondingly, it will be easier to exploit the elements of tacit knowledge if the various items of knowledge and different views can be clarified using drawings or video images, for example. Visualisation will become increasingly important.

Even at this present stage, employees appreciate the opportunities provided by their organisations to update their expertise on a continual basis, and the fact that learning together is part of daily work. The Finnish Association of Graduate Engineers TEK is in the process of testing the EuroRecord tool to survey the competencies of its board members. The EuroRecord is an excellent support in drafting personal study plans, systematic learning, and updating personal CVs.

A point of view: The role of art in knowledge transfer

An extraordinary point of view, which, according to Kilpi, may be too extraordinary, is the growing role of art in knowledge transfer. Kilpi justifies this by the fact that if the Parliament, for example, is presented with a report containing 1,000 pages to be read by tomorrow morning, the situation will be impossible. The gist of the message will disappear in the pile. On the other hand, if the central message could be expressed in the form of images, films or another form of communication emphasising the gist of the message, it would be crucial in future. All employees should be knowledge producers. A human being's capacity to use other than conceptual forms of knowledge is essential. This type of learning and education is important. These activities are not sufficient, or non-existent at present.

To take just one example, the University of Art and Design, Helsinki graduates 12 multimedia experts per year. According to Kilpi, the required amount is between 120 to 1200. "Our businesses and society require huge amounts of this type of expertise. In education political terms, we must be able to identify the requirements of our time. The prevailing conventional view is that if we had an increasing number of people with the ability to generate both explicit and non-explicit knowledge, it would collapse our quality standard. This is not true. In addition, the fear that these people would never be employed is utterly wrong. There is a huge demand for this type of expertise. Even at this early stage, the new type of knowledge literacy is a common theme of discussion, but the development of those skills that are required for knowledge creation will become increasingly essential.

Esko Kilpi, Management Consultant,
Sedecon Consulting

Communities must create and develop opportunities for new high-quality experiences and new high-standard contacts and discussions. Dialogue plays a central role. All people must develop in three regards:

1) experiences,
2) contacts, and
3) interaction.

It is essential to learn to question the existing models constructively on a continual basis. In practice, this refers to leadership, plus models of thought and culture. A culture of openness includes the idea of mutual equality.

Knowledge management is geared towards perceiving the reality of organisations while focusing on knowledge, expertise and learning. Attention must also be paid to the possibilities to increase knowledge, competence and expertise, and to the practical outcomes of these activities.

Work is changing—the production of individual services requires more than mechanical performance

Many conventional occupations are changing in the direction of knowledge work. This is a drastic change that people should become aware of in time, so as to be able to distinguish whether their own work is developing in the same direction. For example, the work and role of a grocery cashier is becoming more versatile.

Grocery cashiers may develop into healthy lifestyle consultants who survey their customers' eating habits and diets. When buying a product, customers actually pay twice: by paying the product price and by allowing their personal acquisition profile to be entered into the shop's database. A customer's acquisition profile data reflects his or

> Responsibility is a central element in knowledge work. Unless individuals are willing to assume personal responsibility for their work, knowledge work cannot be successful.
> **Esko Kilpi, Management Consultant, Sedecon Consulting**

her buying routines, which can be compared to the criteria of healthy food, thus providing the customer with significantly more added value. This will also help to generate discussion—interaction between the cashier and the customer and increase the human aspect. This means that the mere taking of money or processing people's credit cards will not be enough. Instead, a cashier must be able to analyse and produce knowledge for both the customer's and the company's benefit. The production of individual services requires more than a mechanical work performance. Individuals must be responsible and able to act creatively in each specific situation. According to Kilpi, responsibility is one of the crucial elements in knowledge work. Knowledge work cannot be successful unless the individuals are willing to assume personal responsibility for their work. This view will also generate major changes in the activities of the entire organisation. The conventional idea that the management alone is responsible will no longer be feasible.

Knowledge work will replace those work tasks that produce minimal added value. This will also provide more opportunities for individuals to develop and exploit new possibilities in their work and make it personally more sensible. The work communities' work processes will become more versatile, and the role of cooperation emphasised. We live in a world where people's existing competence and expertise is ageing rapidly. Retraining is a must for an increasing number of people on a daily basis. Man's physical or metal capacity does not restrict regeneration, the only impediment is found in people's mental obstacles and their lack of motivation.

Like human relations, businesses and communities are undergoing a continuous process of change. Change invariably brings new challenges for competence and expertise. Unless an organisation is actively engaged in development activities, it will lose its competitiveness. The following issues typically influence progress:

1) What kind of technological development is to be expected for the creation of replacement solutions?
2) What will be the development of competing alternatives for the creation of replacement solutions?
3) What will be the development of customer needs, and what replacement solutions will be required?

> Personal responsibility for one's own competence and expertise and its further development also implies a revision of the employer concept.
> **Esko Kilpi, Management Consultant, Sedecon Consulting**

Personal responsibility and a capability to market and develop one's own competence and expertise are the basics for personal safety and sustainable competitiveness. This applies to all societal sectors, occupations and work tasks alike. People must personally care for the market value of their own competence and expertise, its preservation and further development. Regarding the individual, mental flexibility and a sound self-esteem will be increasingly important. A sound self-esteem is required if an individual is to personally see and cope with his or her own incompleteness.[61]

4.3 Knowledge management from the business point of view

Communities, and businesses in particular, often interpret knowledge management as leadership relating to knowledge and expertise—leadership rather than control since leadership is dynamic, whereas control may be associated with stagnation and the reorganising of existing knowledge.

Results through knowledge

Knowledge management emphasises the dynamic nature of progress, the power of change, and goal-oriented activities towards clearly defined objectives: to obtain results through knowledge.

> Knowledge management emphasises the dynamic nature of progress, the power of change, and goal-oriented activities towards clearly defined objectives: to obtain results through knowledge.
> **Terhi Ogbeide, e-Business Consultant, ICL Invia Oyj**

Even if the business point of view is, naturally, focused on results and profit, it must be borne in mind that knowledge-based results are invariably achieved by people using their own competence and expertise. Therefore, knowledge management refers to expertise management—people management, and the promotion of co-operation. Knowledge is what people accomplish. It is essential to make people co-operate towards the implementation of a shared vision. This means that the sharing of knowledge is the key issue. Throughout the 1990s, the role of co-operation has become increasingly emphasised in business cultures, due to the fact that knowledge-intensive activities focus on networking, jointly produced ideas and expertise development.

Concurrently with the realisation of the importance of co-operation, people have become aware that knowledge is not objective, something detached from the individual, but something connected to action and emotions. In client-oriented

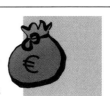

We must change our way of thinking!

In the past: Knowledge is power. I must know!

At present: Knowledge sharing is power. We must know!

Terhi Ogbeide, e-Business Consultant, ICL Invia Oyj

thinking where observing the client's needs and requirements constitutes a competition advantage, a good atmosphere and the will to engage in flexible, seamless co-operation with colleagues become crucial elements.[62]

Knowledge is an asset that need not and must not be saved as it increases through use and wastes away if saved. Knowledge is like joy, which increases and is only revived through unrestricted application.

In the past, knowledge was power that could be kept secret and only used for people's personal goals and for controlling others. Knowledge was possessed by a small group of few selected people. The fewer they were, the greater their power. "With knowledge management ideology as the basis, we must change people's way of thinking to enable them to realise that knowledge sharing is power, and that it is our power," Terhi Ogbeide points out. Is this a new point of view, or does it only mean that the focus has shifted from the individual onto a group, an organisation, or a community pursuing the same interest? Individual and communal responsibility should be intertwined so as to constitute a single entity. The increasing importance of global activities calls for a fundamental re-analysis of the distribution and sharing of responsibility.

A point of view: The Committee for the Future's report refers to the concept of a networking state, a new type of state introduced by Professor Manuel Castells. "A networking state consists of parts of national states, mutual federations on several levels, supranational institutions, regional and local administration units, plus various civic groups and their associations. All these combine into a network of shared responsibility and interaction. (...) In the era of knowledge, our lives, and that of the entire world, will depend on our ability to connect to one another and the network." (Committee for the Future, TuVM 1/1998.)

How to make knowledge effective?

Knowledge can also be distributed without significant effects. An example of this may be the passive knowledge distribution using ICT. Information is made available on the Internet and then people are expected to retrieve it for themselves. In working life, increasing result requirements and tougher competition have led to a situation where people have no time to retrieve and internalise the required knowledge even if it is freely accessible. Knowledge distribution means the sharing of meanings, denotations and connotations. This means that real effective dialogue has undergone a revival. In bygone times, unnecessary discussion and personal interpretations of knowledge were not tolerated at the work place. On the other hand, haste at work may cause the level of knowledge and interaction to remain superficial.

People are still not confident enough to accept that positive, trustful and open co-operation is the best way to achieve results. A shared interest is in everyone's interest. Some may benefit more than or less than others but everyone will get something.

Riitta Korhonen, MP

One of the main aims in knowledge work is to create new knowledge, so it cannot be restricted to the distribution and storage of existing knowledge. People's subjective interpretations are becoming increasingly significant. The functioning of the human mind must be taken seriously. If people only see threats in a pessimistic atmosphere, the will to achieve the agreed objectives will be lost due to a lack of confidence. Positive thinking and belief in joint possibilities have always been the central strengths of people with a mission. It is this energy that organisations endeavour to enhance using various methods.

Learning and working together

One of businesses' central knowledge management objectives is to achieve results through knowledge, to increase the value of the organisation. This cannot be done using ICT alone, due to the fact that technologies need users and users need a knowledge content. For these efforts to be successful, ICT applications and solutions must be tailored in accordance with the client's specific needs and requirements. This objective and work method will require the co-operation skills and creative problem solving capabilities of the designers, builders, sales personnel and content producers involved. The understand-

Apparently, we must create new ways of dividing between work and leisure. Many people would be happy to work uninterrupted for three weeks and then take two weeks off.

Pirjo Ståhle, Professor, Lappeenranta University of Technology

ing, extraction and analysis of client need requires skills and capabilities that were never required in solitary work. The best solutions will be found by working and learning together on a continual basis.[63]

Learning and working together are based on the principle that everybody should win and that the individuals involved are genuinely interested in serving one another. These qualities are feasible for man but they will not emerge through force, nor do they flourish in an atmosphere dominated by competition, envy and people being threatened by having an insufficient or rapidly ageing personal competence. Regarding the individual, knowledge management, knowledge creation and client-oriented thinking will require increasing self-initiative and responsibility for the development of his or her own competence and expertise. More often than not, the individual in question is also required to learn an entirely new occupation, with the creation of a new work culture. This also means that work communities, and especially their leaders, will be responsible for the organisation's continual intellectual growth. This type of entrepreneurship idea is, nevertheless, largely contradictory to the conventional idea of paid employment. Consequently, work must be mentally rewarding, well paid, or mission-based, for people to genuinely reach the objective. The redundancy threat will keep people awake and active but the costs will be high, due to work-related exhaustion and long sick leaves.

Sharing and dissemination of knowledge

 Do not kill an emerging idea! This sentence by Ikujiro Nonaka illustrates a daily challenge encountered by every knowledge-intensive organisation, in the private and public sectors alike. Knowledge management—the knowledge leadership skill—is geared towards the elimination of those impediments that used to keep work cultures unenthusiastic, over-critical or indifferent. Brainstorming is generated through genuine interest and dialogue, and by continuously learning to share other people's ideas, instead of knocking them down as stupid suggestions. The distribution, application and tailoring of knowledge also require a cultural change to take place within the organisation in question. Keeping knowledge secret, or a work culture where everybody only minds their own business, will be unacceptable, provided that the company's competitiveness depends on what its capable employees can develop and learn together.

In addition to being client-oriented, an organisation's or a group of company's operations must be internally interactive. Nevertheless, it is very common for people not to know what others are doing. Knowledge sharing and dissemination is necessary but difficult. It will require time, independent thinking and a skill to sum up the essentials. People must learn to tell others what they are aware of, in a form that attracts other people's interest.

> The important issue of knowledge sharing and knowledge dissemination has always caused problems in the Finnish language, due to the fact that they both translate into a single equivalent in our language. However, sharing and dissemination are two separate things. Knowledge management requires both.
> **Merja Karivalo, Training Manager, Helsinki University of Technology, Lifelong Learning Institute Dipoli**

Innovative activities always include selling the idea in question, even if it were not considered a separate work task. A novelty always includes a certain amount of uncertainty. Therefore, it is important in the dissemination process that the communication takes place as part of an interactive process. One-way communication is not sufficient. Mechanical communication may turn into interaction if at least one of the two parties is familiar with the new product or service, has tested it or taken it into use.

Dissemination is more than marketing, communicating or informing. A social change does not take place in a moment, and therefore it is important to be aware of the process-like character of dissemination. The idea has to be sold slowly so that the customers will have time to get used to the idea of accepting it. Dissemination is influencing.[64]

 **The definition of dissemination:** Dissemination (diffusion) is an interactive process with the help of which the participants create and deliver information to each other about an innovation in order to reach mutual understanding. Successful dissemination of an innovation produces change in people's thinking and actions. Dissemination always consists of four recognisable and definable elements: Innovation, dissemination channels, time, and the people and communities, which form the social system of the dissemination process. (Rogers 1983.)

According to research, the greatest part by far of an innovation causes only a slight change in the total demand or in the behaviour of consumers. Habits, attitudes and values as well as financial and cultural factors all contribute to the willingness to adopt innovations. This can be clearly seen in learning, too. According to the innovative concept of learning, learning is not devoid of values, and values change very slowly. While this is an obstacle to progress, it also has a protective effect. Excessive enthusiasm for novelties can also lead to a development that is not desirable.[65]

The following items are included in a report on the Finnish Government's political decisions which emphasise the importance of dissemination and its comprehensive content:

• The purpose of an innovation system is to create preconditions for the exploitation of knowledge and know-how by individuals, society and the national economy. Its development is to focus on strengthening people's preconditions to exploit knowledge and know-how.

• An individual's preparedness and ability to learn new things are the key issues in the exploitation of knowledge and know-how. They constitute the basis for all exploitation, the individuals' appropriate subsistence and their intellectual growth. They are also the basis for successful practical lifelong learning.

• Exploitation has become increasingly actual in all societal development activities with diversifying functions and the focus of development efforts increasingly shifting from quantitative onto qualitative development through profitability considerations and target definitions.

• The dissemination and exploitation of knowledge and know-how is increasingly dependent on interaction where knowledge production, transfer, acquisition and exploitation take place in close networking co-operation. Expanding and delving more deeply into network co-operation activities has become a key issue in the development of our national innovation system.

(Science and Technology Policy Council of Finland, 1996.)

Creating knowledge through work

Work is continually subjected to new objectives and requirements and people learn together when putting these into practice. Working together makes people sensitive to the perception of new points of view and results in the finding of joint energy. This emotion helps participants commit themselves and endure the continual chaos that is generated by an uninterrupted flow of new information. Work is used to generate new theory that is subsequently reacted to through continued work. People can share meanings and knowledge by working together. When people share knowledge they also share power. An authorised person is responsible and committed to co-operation.

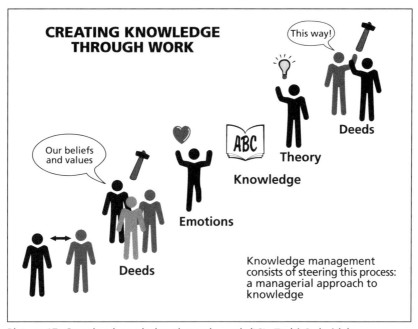

Picture 17: Creating knowledge through work (ICL, Terhi Ogbeide).

The purpose of knowledge management is to achieve results through knowledge and increase the value of the organisation involved. All knowledge management solutions are different. Each community should independently consider what is relevant for it to know and understand. The customer and the supplier should jointly survey their knowledge management needs and resolve the challenges together.

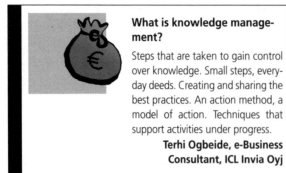

What is knowledge management?

Steps that are taken to gain control over knowledge. Small steps, everyday deeds. Creating and sharing the best practices. An action method, a model of action. Techniques that support activities under progress.

Terhi Ogbeide, e-Business Consultant, ICL Invia Oyj

Each organisation can find the solution within itself. External help is required to ask questions and provide new perspectives. Information systems are to be developed with the needs as their basis.

A company-specific solution

As such, an organisation contains a wealth of knowledge, both explicit and tacit knowledge. The problem in knowledge management is to put the organisation's existing knowledge to use, not only to be shared but to be used as extensively as possible. Knowledge cannot increase or create new knowledge until somebody uses somebody else's knowledge.

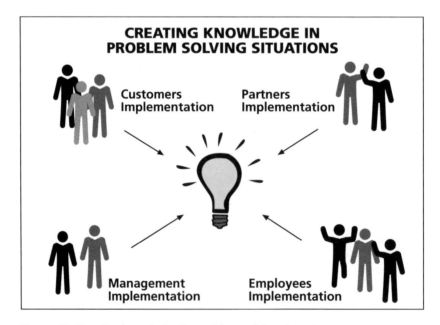

Picture 18: Creating knowledge in problem solving situations (ICL, Terhi Ogbeide).

ICL is a company that embarked on developing its own knowledge management based on the Internet. International teams pondered over feasible methods to make knowledge and knowledge assets accessible to everyone. There is such a huge number and range of projects in progress globally, that mere information is not sufficient to keep people up to date on what is being done and developed elsewhere.

International teams are engaged in developing central knowledge management processes, communities, roles and the related essential knowledge. One of the main joint achievements is a database used to describe relevant project-related matters for the information of others. Everyone can easily access and update this database with information from his or her project. In addition, joint bulletin boards are used for project enquiries and to exchange experiences.

The organisation's database includes, in most cases, only the basic information of different projects and other activities. This information is, but the tip of the iceberg, consisting of the organisation's knowledge and expertise. However, daily work is required to maintain this information in a form that is easily accessible, work that tends to be neglected in haste. A lot of work is required to interest people in knowledge sharing and dialogue since this consumes time and energy. For example, people must thoroughly understand the benefits of sharing tacit knowledge, prior to investing time in it. Dialogue will make the existing in-depth expertise, which is continually used by various projects, more widely known throughout the organisation. It will also process it into shared wisdom. To achieve real dialogue or learning interaction, people must encounter others and realise the rewarding nature of sharing their own knowledge, on the one hand, and that of building on the knowledge of other people, on the other.

ICL Invia Oyj and the Sonera Corporation are both companies where the personnel are engaged in active dialogue and in analysing what is significant knowledge for the purpose of knowledge creation.[66]

ICL, in particular, offers business applications based on Internet technology for the needs of major businesses and public administration. The company's central business includes e-business solutions that are integrated into basic applications and industry-specific systems and require the support of an information technological infrastructure. ICL designs, implements and operates applications for each of these fields.

Innovation—the basis for regeneration

According to research, as much as 95% of a company's value consists of intangible assets. In an intangible competition environment, innovation and expertise are crucial elements for

Processing the deluge of information will help people get the general drift.

Pirjo Ståhle, Professor, Lappeenranta University of Technology

success. In the early 1990s, a new theory of growth indicated that economic growth is generated by competition between companies, and that the capability of continuous innovation would be the most important means of business success. Innovation, i.e. novelty or reform, is a more extensive concept than invention as it also contains thoughts and insights, for example. What is typical of competition in a new, third wave economy, is that organisations can use technological development to raise people's knowledge to a considerably higher level.[67]

Pirjo Ståhle describes the birth of an innovation as follows: Initially, a significant amount of varying, even contradictory information is required. Experts from various fields tend to think differently. They all have their own truth, language and view. Hearing several viewpoints on the issue at hand calls one's own perspective into question or makes it more versatile. This leads to confusion and chaos in one's mind. Processing the deluge of information helps one get the general drift. People recognise this state of clarification—new ideas emerge.

Following the innovation stage, people must carry on with the ordinary project work. If a company is not capable of converting the results into products, innovation cannot help it succeed in competition. (Talouselämä 24/2000.)

> Let's take the example of interpreting a telephone conversation between two people who are a long physical distance apart from one another. How do different people interpret this event?
>
> • A technical interpretation by an engineer: Transmission of electrical impulses. In principle these are digitally encoded variations in air pressure.
>
> • A symbolic interpretation by a linguist: Transmission of speech in the Finnish language.
>
> • A commercial interpretation by an economist: Transmission of marketable messages.
>
> • A cultural interpretation by a sociologist: Transmission of meanings and connotations, conducting a discourse.
>
> • A practical interpretation by a user: Putting life into practice with the purpose of sharing it with another person.
>
> (The Ministry of Labour 1999.)

Innovation invariably refers to the organisation's ability to benefit from its self-organisation. For innovations to emerge, various issues must be given ample space to independently find their form. **Ilya Prigogine,** an American Nobel Prize Winner, defined four universal principles that manifest themselves in all self-regenerating systems. According to Pirjo Ståhle and **Mauri Grönroos,** innovations only emerge if the following four criteria are fulfilled:

1. Innovation is based on chaos.
2. For an innovation to emerge, a huge amount of information is eventually required.
3. Innovation requires sensitivity to perceive weak signals.
4. Innovation has a timescale of its own.

"Chaos invariably arouses feelings of insecurity and confusion. This means that they are an inseparable part of the innovation capability."[68]

Added value of knowledge

From the point of view of profitability and employment, the knowledge application method and the consequent production method may be at entirely different levels. Extending knowledge to cover the cause and effect of the process, as well as understanding the processes in various conjunctions will increase opportunities to generate added value in business. This, in turn, is the precondition for sustainable employment in a market economy. ICT or the elementary components of knowledge cannot, as such, constitute a sufficient basis for generating added value.[69]

Level of knowledge	Form of knowledge	Apllicability to production process	Added value
data	saving storing	raw material	+ +
informaatio	encoding		
tieto	transferring analysing explaining	duplicating processing innovative	++ +++ ++++

In addition, there must be a business idea and its implementation. Work organisations must also develop ideas and disseminate solutions on a continual basis. This will fail, if people cannot interpret knowledge. People must become aware of why things are the way they are, and what conditions the knowledge refers to. This means the production of subsequent innovations pertaining to the business idea in question. The more the work processes contain such qualities that increase events on the level of explaining and understanding, the greater the added value and potential employment achieved.[70]

The difficulty lies, not in the new ideas, but in escaping from the old ones, which ramify, for those brought up as most of us have been, into every corner of our minds.

Keynes 1936

A point of view: Knowledge management starts with the goals of the company.

In the constantly changing world, companies must keep on their toes and they must be able to adjust to unexpected things. One must even know what one does not know.

Knowledge management is a process by which information is created, acquired, shared and utilised. "At first one must chart out carefully what information is really needed by the company and how to manage that information in order to obtain the maximum use from it", says Esa Tihilä, the manager of the ICL Electronic Business department.

A good starting point is the organisation's goals, visions and mission. "The significance of the information to each sector is decisive. And it is not enough that we get information about our own company, we need information about our network partners, such as the most important clients and principals."

In fact companies already have information, in fact they are being overwhelmed by information. The problem is to know how to pick from the mass the essential points and the information that best serves the different groups.

"Information systems are important, but it has been found that they are by no means in a crucial position in knowledge management. What is more important is to have the understanding, the will and the skill to share information with others."

When we know what we know and know how to utilise what we know, we are able to buildseamless knowledge management chains extending from the suppliers to the clients and back again. "When all the memos and minutes are stored safely, resources are manageable and the needed information easily found. Information flows freely and concrete, valuable benefits are gained through a well-managed system, for example, lead-times become shorter."

www.icl.fi

4.4 Knowledge management from a societal and regional point of view

From a regional point of view, knowledge management is comparable to interaction between individuals and communities. Regional policy decisions are used to enable an increasing number of organisations to participate in innovative environments and more open interaction with other organisations and businesses. Centres of this type are self-sustaining.

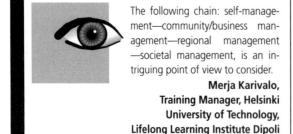

The following chain: self-management—community/business management—regional management—societal management, is an intriguing point of view to consider.

Merja Karivalo,
Training Manager, Helsinki
University of Technology,
Lifelong Learning Institute Dipoli

Castells (1996) describes the new economic order as informational and global. The new society is a networking society where the central functions are increasingly network-based. Network participation and network dynamics are critical sources of power.

Four all-permeating success factors for Finland's future, and the cycle of social well-being

In its 1997 report (TuV1/1997), the Committee for the Future defined four all-permeating success factors for Finland's future, all of which may have an increasing, effect and importance not just on national policy, but especially at the regional level:

1) Wisely influencing globalisation,
2) Exploiting information and technology to the full,
3) The human aspect in innovation and
4) Governance of matters and life.

In its 1998 report (Committee for the Future, TuVM 1/1998), the Committee for the Future deals with the cycle of social well-being where the factors bearing on social well-being are interdependent. The movement of wealth is crucial for this cycle to function. The relationship between the wealth increasing factors and the parties responsible for those factors must be in good order. If any one basic factor limps along, the whole system limps along.

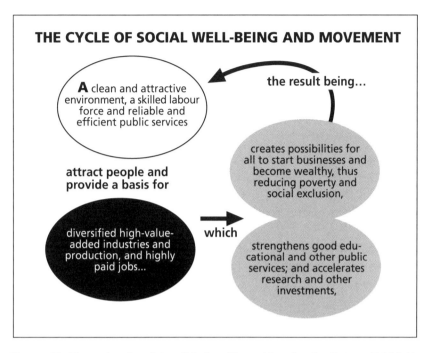

Picture 19: The cycle of social well-being (Committee for the Future, TuVM 1/ 1998).

Efficient and productive labour, a good living environment, a well-educated populace, efficient public services and an enterprising, innovative atmosphere make Finland an excellent location for businesses and, above all, for the enterprises that will perform the demanding work of the future. These are the qualities that innovative, successful environments are famous for. However, people's ideas of success vary a great deal. Busy development centres are not to everyone's liking. Instead, they may prefer a peaceful life with access to the required services without having to stand in queues. This may become a crucial factor when choosing a living environment. However, even these areas are often connected to development centres, which means that co-operation between various areas becomes the decisive element. A delegation from our TA Project made a visit to Oulu where several local speakers emphasised that the wealth and well-being of the southern area around Oulu, for example, is strongly dependent on the success of Oulu City in many respects.

Learning regions are successful in a changing world

In a new learning-oriented economy, the most important success factor in economic competition is knowledge, with learning being the most important process. Therefore, the challenge is: How to create a competitive action environment for lifelong learning and the creation of new expertise and innovations. According to Väyrynen (1999), urban areas will be increasingly responsible for the development of learning action environments. This is due to the fact that, in a global world, the state can only have restricted means to influence their development. Consequently, the state's role will mainly be restricted to providing encouragement to declining areas using a number of direct and indirect methods. Business Development Director **Juha Kostiainen** (2000) has carried out research into the urban areas of Helsinki, Oulu and Tampere as innovative milieus. According to him, development policies are currently undergoing an increasing shift of focus from subvention to competitiveness.[71]

Research into innovative environments was launched in the mid-1980s when the GREMI group (Groupe de Recherche Européen sur les Milieux Innovateurs) was established. The group has carried out research into technological innovations and the development of innovative regions in the spirit of **Philippe Aydalot,** its founder: "A business is not an operation that has fallen from the sky, one that could freely choose its environment, but one that is "embedded" in its environment: it is the milieu that takes the initiative and is innovative (…) Thus, the hypothesis is that the local milieu has a central role as a creator of innovations, a prism that is penetrated by innovation efforts (…) A business is not an isolated innovative operation but part of a milieu that enables the business to operate. The main components of innovations include the regions' history, their organisation, collective behaviour and their underlying consensus."[72]

Based on the researchers' various definitions, Kostiainen sums up the central characteristics of an innovative milieu as follows:

- A milieu is part of a geographic area.
- Interaction between various active parties plays the central role. This is based on proximity, a shared culture, reciprocity and trust.
- A milieu is outwardly open and acquires complementary knowledge and expertise from the outside world.
- A milieu generates synergy and collective learning.
- In a milieu, working relationships are often networks and networks "emerge" from the milieu.

What is central in the development of innovative milieus is their activation, which enables bi-directional activities according to Maillat (1995): in order to develop interactive logic and dynamic learning. Regarding interactive logic, it is essential to concentrate on developing the type of co-operation that is geared towards producing innovations that generate innovation networks in due course. The dynamics of learning, in turn, describe the operators' ability to adapt their activities to the changes taking place in the environment over the course of time. At the practical level, the developing of learning dynamics means, for example, producing new expertise, defining new forms for the regulation of activities, and providing education and training.[73]

Autio (2000) has carried out research into two innovative regions that differ markedly from each other—Sophia Antipolis in southern France and the Otaniemi region in Espoo, Finland. According to research results, new technological businesses gain substantial learning benefits from regional concentration. These benefits manifest themselves as physical proximity enabling the businesses to build their social capital with the central interest group relations as the basis. The research indicated that there is no single correct approach to building an innovative milieu. Instead, a wide variety of solutions may prove to be functional in practice. In the long-term, with regard to competition between regions, successful regions seemed to be those that had such a culture and innovation systems that inspire learning in local businesses and support entrepreneur-driven innovation processes. The more the region's institutional structures could support learning and the testing of new ideas, the more dynamic and more capable of change appeared the regional economy. As Autio sees it, learning regions have the best preconditions for success in a world undergoing a process of change.[74]

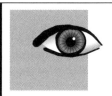

The Silicon Valley model is based on inhumane competition with suicide, alcoholism and drug abuse being the other side of the coin. Therefore, this is not an advisable model. A much repeat statement in researcher meetings has been: Yes, it's terrible, but are there any alternatives? Now, I tell them that the alternative is Finland!

Manuel Castells, Professor, University of California Berkeley

Learning and a company's social capital

In theory, a company's learning is based on two mechanisms: communication and combination. Communication is required for the transfer of knowledge: the more efficiently a

Knowledge can be converted into valuable expertise, provided that it is closely connected to its social context.

company communicates internally and between other companies, the more likely it is that people learn. The combination of knowledge, in turn, generates actual learning events, which means the creation of new organisational knowledge. The knowledge combination process essentially depends on the functionality of the transfer process: if knowledge transfer fails, no opportunities can be created for the combination of various knowledge elements.[75]

Researchers say that one of the most significant insights made in strategic research during the late 1990s was the realisation of the social nature of businesses. It is essential for the existence of businesses to have the capacity to generate, store and exploit knowledge in various social contexts. A social frame of reference provides knowledge with meaning, while the processes of knowledge creation, storage and exploitation are based on social interaction. Knowledge can be converted into valuable expertise, provided that it is closely connected to its social context. Stock exchange expertise is probably more valuable in the City of London than in the rain forests of Borneo, for example.[76]

The significance of social capital as a regulator of central regeneration processes in businesses is explained by the social nature of knowledge, expertise and businesses. Autio summarises a company's social capital as "whom you know". This is the quality that separates social capital from human capital that, in a business, consists of "what you know". There is an intensive interaction between social capital and human capital.

Regarding interaction between businesses and their leaders, Nahapiet and Ghoshal (1998) identify three main dimensions. Each of these must be taken into account when pondering on what steps to take for the creation of innovative and growth-oriented regional milieus. Mere networking (a structural dimension) will not be sufficient. The proportional (relational) and cognitive dimensions must also be taken into account.

The significance of social capital as a regulator of central regeneration processes in businesses is explained by the social nature of knowledge, expertise and businesses.

The structural dimension of social capital is an indication of a company's internal and external networks. It indicates the customers, suppliers, and other external and internal interest groups who the company in question is networked with. The structural dimension indicates the amount of various existing connections, as well as the type of the network's organisation and hierarchy.

However, this dimension does not indicate how the network in question operates in reality. The proportional dimension of social capital regulates the level of intimacy, openness and confidence of the interest group relations, and how well these function in practice. The more open and confidential the interest group relations are, the more flexible and efficient are the dissemination of knowledge and ideas. The proportional dimension of social capital ensures that the various parties can trust one another to such a degree that they are prepared to share even confidential knowledge and information. This is done in a fashion that provides the maximum learning benefits from interest group relations. People also use these sustaining personal relations to satisfy their social needs, such as gaining social appreciation and approval by others. For a network to support a regional innovative milieu, for example, it must not only exist but also provide its members with opportunities to satisfy their needs for social interaction.

For a network to support a regional innovative milieu, for example, it must not only exist but also provide its members with opportunities to satisfy their needs for social interaction.

The cognitive dimension of social capital regulates the efficiency of communication in interest group relations. The parties understand one another, in other words, they speak the same language. However, creating the required structure and ensuring the network's functionality will not be enough. What is also required is that the knowledge content is correct and relevant to the users.

Creating expertise-based competitive advantages by learning together

Yli-Renko, Autio and Sapienza tested the predictive power of the social capital theory to explain the development of expertise-based competitive advantages in new technological businesses (a total of 180 new technological businesses) in the U.K. The research outcome indicated that the various components of social capital were, to a statistically significant degree, dependent on learning from key customer relationships. The said learning explains the generation of competition advantages as well as that of any dependence-related adverse effects. A significant observation was that the effect of social capital on the generation of an expertise-based competitive advantage is entirely conveyed through learning. In other words, social capital, as such, does not explain the generation of an expertise-based competitive advantage. Instead, learning from a customer relationship is the critical mediating factor in this process. The diagram below shows how the structural component of social capital, in particular, explains learning from customer relationships. On the other hand, the quality of customer relationships, which was analysed during the research in conjunction with relative and cognitive factors, proved to be negative with regard to learning together.

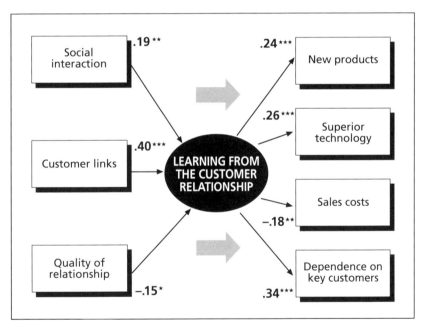

Picture 20: Social capital, learning from a key-customer relationship, and expertise-based competitive advantage (Autio 2000.)

The diagram summaries the results of the statistical structural analysis and the variables used in the research. The variables of social capital are shown on the left, with learning advantages gained by new technological businesses from their key customers shown in the middle. The expertise-based competitive advantage factors and the technological businesses' dependence on their key-customers are shown on the right.

According to Autio, the close location of suppliers to their customers has been found to be beneficial in the building of social capital. This partly explains why new technological businesses want to establish themselves in regional centres. Even if communication is partly possible through various technical media, ICT solutions still seem incapable of conveying the type valuable, experience-based knowledge or tacit knowledge that is crucial for gaining a competitive advantage. Telephones or e-mail cannot enable the creation of such confidential relations that the parties involved would be ready to use them to communicate their most valuable and confidential information, pertaining to new technological projects, or their product development projects.[77]

The research also indicated that a company's competitive advantage was not generated by its negotiating power arising from a close geographic location, or by cost efficiency due to joint purchasing functions—it was generated by learning. The main message is that new technological businesses gain substantial learning benefits from regional concentration. These benefits manifest themselves as physical proximity that enables the businesses to build their social capital with the central interest group relations as the basis.

Telework—an information society paradox?

In an information society, the possibility of working anywhere at any time has been regarded as a significant issue from the regional point of view. This means that telework would increase the freedom of choice for individuals and businesses alike. However, recent research results indicate that the close physical proximity between various parties and operators will intensify the building of social capital, and the exploitation of external sources of learning. This generates an information society paradox: the location factors have become increasingly important for business activities, regardless of the fact that ICT could, in principle, allow many business activities to be conducted anywhere at any time. According to Autio, the influence of social capital on learning, regarding businesses and individuals alike, also explains why reaching the telework objectives, for example, has failed to a large extent.

In reality, knowledge workers did not move to the countryside and start teleworking from their summerhouses. On the contrary, it is the most competent labour force with the best expertise that is most eagerly moving to the centres of growth as these provide superior location-based learning benefits, compared to remote rural areas.

The possibility of avoiding disturbance in one's work environment has been regarded as a classic motive for telework. The phone does not keep on ringing and there are no "disturbing" customers bothering you, and you can work whenever you please. The possibility to concentrate on work in an entirely different environment, such as at home, a summerhouse, or a library, has also been considered as a motivating factor. Telework requires personal qualities, such as self-discipline and independence, plus the possibility of using the required tools and fast Internet connections. (78) Naturally, it is paradoxical that telework was thought to be the solution to save the declining municipalities and villages, whereas, on the other hand, communication and learning together are constantly emphasised as the personal success factors for knowledge professionals.

According to Kilpi, a challenge to regional development in an information society is to ensure a sufficient quality of life and technological infrastructure for those people who live part of their lives, which may be a major part, away from the centres of growth.

Knowledge management is not only a technical issue but also a political one. The building of an information society is too often considered to be just a technical issue. In fact, most of the decisive choices are frequently political. The building of a wireless mobile phone network (3rd generation mobile phones) is an example of a multidimensional political decision made in the sphere of knowledge management. Until now, Finland has been among the pioneers. NMT phones came to the Nordic Countries in the 1980s, the world's first GSM operator permits were granted here in 1990, and the first commercial GSM call was made in the same year. In March, 1999, Finland granted the world's first 3rd generation operator permits to four applicants. It may be said that Finland chose a policy that may be called a Linus model as it is also based on the principle of unrestricted distribution free of charge. This principle is considered as essential for the field's future development In this case, the market is expected to help the best technology win in mutual competition, and to cater for the consumers' and society's interests. The state did not consider itself competent to choose a specific technology as superior to all others. Choosing the wrong technology may be fatal.

Finland decided not to sell permits at a high price, not to arrange an auction, nor to allow the winner to do what he pleases, even regarding the future pricing of services. The state bases its decisions on fair competition but retains control over the situation—in cases where the operators do not fulfil specific requirements regarding development, pricing, democracy, or any other significant aspect, the permit conditions may be revised or cancelled.

Most other European states have amassed huge profits from permit sales, mainlythrough auctions. It has been asked why the State of Finland refused the so-called easy money. Which is the best way a) in the short term or b) in the long term? Which model will ensure open competition for the best technology in future?

Paula Tiihonen, Committee Counsellor

As a nation, can we successfully develop, and approve the required steps to be taken on all central levels of decision-making and activities, in order to establish knowledge-based expertise as the basis for regional well-being, economic wealth, and intellectual growth, in particular, in our country? It is not advisable to base information networks on wide-band connections, or to invest heavily in them, unless there are enthusiastic users to produce the type of content that can attract increasing enthusiasm. Undisputedly, the state and the municipalities can accelerate the desired societal development trends in many ways. Nevertheless, the most decisive element will be found in people's personal enthusiasm and their will to consume a significant portion of their own time to create new, insight-based knowledge using new ICT tools. This refers to people's leisure time activities and to developing new product and service ideas for the global market.

The TA Steering Group members familiarised themselves with innovative milieus

The TA Steering Group visited innovative milieus in Helsinki, Oulu and Jyväskylä in Finland, and Boston (a local knowledge and expertise cluster), Washington D.C. (an administration cluster), the Silicon Valley, California (a cluster of new business activities) in the U.S.A. In addition to the TA Steering Group members and secretaries, a number of external experts were also invited. On the "Silicon Hill" of Helsinki (Pitäjänmäki), the role of new technology and its development through co-operation between networked businesses were emphasised. ICL, Sonera and Nokia are among the companies involved in continuous co-operation to develop the region. In addition to high-capacity Internet connections, a house of technology, for example, with the required infrastructure available for versatile, efficient electronic communication has been built.

The strong growth and success of businesses in the Oulu region indicated that even smaller areas are capable of success. The ways and means to succeed include, for example, marketing the correct models of action, plus the financial arrangements to provide the businesses with the correct type of funding.

What was also emphasised was the role of education and training in support of new technology and competitiveness in the global market. An example was the Pohto Electronic Industry Training Factory that was established as a result of the Pro Electronica Project launched by the Oulu Region Centre of Excellence Programme. This project is geared towards raising Finnish electronic production expertise to the global top level. Regarding regional development, there is generally an active core (a person, a community, etc.) that launches networking activities, summaries an issue, enables people to develop their identity, etc.[79] A prime example of this in the Oulu region is the Pyhäjoki Upper secondary school specialised in entrepreneurship where students publish a small regional newspaper Students are instructed to use new technology, they are introduced to the reality of entrepreneurship in practice and encouraged to participate in the activities of their own community as responsible operators.

The Jyväskylä Centre of Technology also emphasised the strong growth trend of small businesses as providers of new employment, and the importance of entrepreneurship for the entire nation's success. Various practical examples were used to illustrate the variety of the knowledge management perspective. At times, the visitors were not absolutely sure whether the hosts were specifically referring to knowledge management or just the general development of businesses and society.

The field trip to the U.S.A was designed with the purpose of enabling the Committee for the Future to become acquainted with three largely differing knowledge management targets. Boston is a conventional model of success based on engineering. The basis is provided by strong universities (Harvard and MIT). These have always had close and functional connections to business life. It has been feared that California will beat the region, especially in competition for investments. In the long term, however, its strength is seen in basic research and long-standing investments.

In Washington D.C., state-conducted information society projects continue to be important, like the associated think tanks and influential civic groups. In addition to commercial politics, state projects are used to cater for the citizens' equality, education and training, the general atmosphere, and taxation. With regard to business activities, the region has gained a more significant role over the past few years. Around the nation's capital, a dynamic cluster of high tech businesses, electronic businesses in particular, has emerged in less than 10 years.

The Silicon Valley is an incredible concentration of the new economy located along Highway 101. The Silicon Valley is a model example of an innovative milieu that everyone wants to be close to. While the new economy provides enormous opportunities for both small and large companies alike, the region's living standard is continually rising, with an increasing gap opening between the rich and the poor.

There are certain differences between the Finnish and the American attitude towards knowledge management, networking and co-operation. While we are often compelled to build shared structures and comprehensive co-operation due to our limited resources; the American model pays distinctively more attention to commercial structures, strategic and selective co-operation and the importance of mutually competitive solutions. These are the very reasons why public intervention is still strongly opposed. As a professor from the Stanford University said "the Finnish system was designed by engineers, so it works like a machine. Whereas the U.S.A is like a rain forest where anything can grow big".[80]

In several respects, Finland is a pioneer of information society development. Important characteristics, which are typical of Finland, include the citizens' wide and enthusiastic use of mobile phones and the Internet, and opportunities provided to almost all citizens to participate in networked activities. Nevertheless, new technological methods and services, in particular, are only generated, to a significant degree, under circumstances where business activities flourish, there is a plentiful provision of services and products in the field, and these are bought at market prices. Regarding electronic trade and business activities, the U.S.A. is the undisputed leader.

Thoughts aroused by our wide ranging and rewarding visit to the U.S.A.:

1) The idea that Finland and the Nordic Countries should have a special advantage regarding the division of labour in a so-called global innovation system in its experimental stage, is fascinating. This emerged during our visit to the Institute for the Future (Palo Alto, CA). I believe Finland has made the correct political decisions to become the leading

developer of technology in specific fields, but could the citizens' general willingness to adopt innovations be used to build something new?

2) The message from MIT and Harvard is: visions are significant for the orientation of research in a rapidly changing world. This is a lesson for Finland. Maybe we should even reform our universities to enable the production of researchers with increased visionary capabilities?

3) If Finland is as good as our host suggested, how can the country retain its current position and develop it on a continual basis? We can no longer adopt external models, we must have the vision, boldness, courage and wisdom to develop a "leading strategy" of our own.

Eija Ahola, Unit Manager, National Technology Agency TEKES

In the activities of the Committee for the Future, innovations in general, and social innovations in particular, are seen as national success factors. The TA Steering Group wanted to delve into these issues, and especially into regional innovation activities to a considerably larger extent than was possible in practice. This means that the summary report accepted by the Committee for the Future includes several proposals for action pertaining to these issues.

The Committee for the Future's TA Steering Group made an educational visit to the U.S.A. that established good contacts to local research centres and educational institutions, for example. In addition to co-operating with leading universities, it would be appropriate for Finland, regarding its global role, to launch projects monitored by the Committee, the results of which would also be used in parliamentary work, for example in conjunction with the World Bank's knowledge management projects and those launched by the Institute for the Future Studies and the University of Santa Clara, Silicon Valley, concentrating on analysing ethical questions in information society development.

TA Steering Group

5. Values and learning—building a shared reality

Knowledge creates new knowledge. Knowledge work will involve increasing inno-vativeness requirements. The number of jobs based on mechanical repetition will decrease and will increasingly be replaced by work that is mentally more demand-ing. The profile of a knowledge professional consists of knowledge, expertise and wisdom. With an increasing amount of knowledge-intensive work in a working community, an individual will have an increasing responsibility regarding his or her own skills and expertise. Organisations will have to analyse what knowledge means to the community, what type of added value it produces, where the commu-nity's knowledge capital resides, and how to measure, evaluate and develop intan-gible capital assets.

New technology has a major impact on the volume of knowledge, and on its processing methods. According to experts, the increasing extent of change and the possibilities for action provided to people, plus global activities, will impose in-creasing requirements on technological development and its exploitation. This will increase the pressure for learning and developing co-operation cultures.

Innovativeness generates innovativeness - but only in a trustworthy and trusting environment. To be reliable, one must rely on others. It is only in a trusting work-ing community, which equally appreciates various expertise contributions by dif-ferent employees, that the entire available expertise capacity can be successfully exploited and increased. Asking and questioning are also important in a future work culture. New methods must be developed for leadership, practical lifelong learning, networking, and co-operation between the public and private sectors. People can no longer be led using the methods of an industrialised society. They have to modernise their work methods and become aware of the underlying values in their activities. In the capacity of a knowledge user and knowledge creator, the individual will always be at the focal point of knowledge management.

During our Technology Assessment Project, a number of knowledge manage-ment concepts emerged as focal points from the perspective of knowledge work. These are learning, values and innovative, responsible utilisation of the methods and opportunities provided by the knowledge society. What we emphasise are those elements that appear to be ignored and neglected in knowledge work, regardless of the fact that they are frequently highlighted when speaking about knowledge management. For example, as learning individuals faced with the challenge of implementing his or her own lifelong learning processes, people are easily taken for granted without further analysis. The implementation methods and opportunities available for lifelong learning are so abundant that their non-existence cannot be the issue.

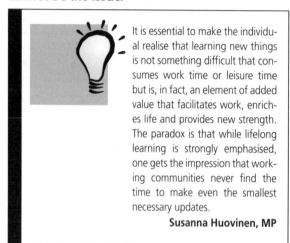

It is essential to make the individual realise that learning new things is not something difficult that consumes work time or leisure time but is, in fact, an element of added value that facilitates work, enriches life and provides new strength. The paradox is that while lifelong learning is strongly emphasised, one gets the impression that working communities never find the time to make even the smallest necessary updates.

Susanna Huovinen, MP

During the TA Project, we pondered the ways, means and views required to convert our current knowledge management practices into a method of action that could continually help individuals and organisations create new knowledge and regenerate themselves. To be able to analyse our work and clarify our views we used the Knowledge Management Dynamo concept as a tool. This concept has been developed and used by Riitta Suurla and Markku Markkula in Finnish and international projects on lifelong learning and organisational change projects.

Defining values and changing them into a progressive series of determined action is always a long and difficult process. The KM Dynamo with its various phases provides a model for developing a working community in a holistic and analysed fashion. Each phase will require new and sustaining steps to be carried out.

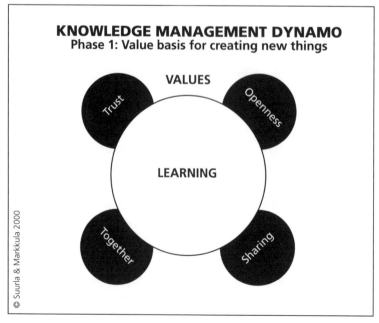

Picture 21: KM Dynamo, phase 1. Value basis for the creation of new things.

5.1 Values

Phase one of the Knowledge Management Dynamo is used to describe trust and openness as the basic knowledge management values. The work methods and practical values are sharing,

The internalisation of values requires the identification and appreciation of basic values. Man is never complete."
Riitta Korhonen, MP

doing together and learning together. These values have been identified as the knowledge management prerequisites by many sectors and parties who have been challenged for extensive KM development and, as well, to put these values into effect on a long run. Values are the highest principles that steer all action and decision-making. This means that they contain the vision of the knowledge society. Provided that knowledge management is geared towards wisdom, as the literature in the field instructs, we must keep these values alive in practice. Values are inherent in goal-oriented learning, i.e. the passion to learn. This is the heart of the KM Dynamo that keeps the Dynamo functioning on a continual basis.

Values provide a challenge to individuals, communities and society. Values must be processed consciously on each

Values have a double role. They describe the real direction of activities and indicate what to aim at.

level. Learning resides in the heart of the Dynamo combining the basic values and method-related values. In knowledge-intensive work, learning cannot be the responsibility of the individual alone. For a learning-oriented individual to work with an innovative spirit with others, he or she must possess trust and openness as his or her genuine personal values. In addition, we must understand that sharing and helping others will benefit the entire organisation or community involved. Doing and learning together are not restricted to working together. The knowledge creation process introduced by Nonaka is only successful if people can surpass their limits as individuals and as a group, and thus learn continuously together (see Chapter 3). We must learn how to surpass our limits. Drafting ideas with others, mutual help, support and encouragement are good methods in this work.

Learning-oriented individuals excel themselves

In knowledge work, a learning-oriented individual constitutes the focal point for knowledge management. We use knowledge to convince ourselves and other people.[81] Doing things to-

Values are the small number of central and enduring principles that guide all aspects of our behaviour.

(Wickens 1999.)

gether requires that we influence one another, share ideas and discuss new points of view. But this also requires that we are ready to be convinced, that is to listen to other people and weigh up their views. We must personally strive to maximise our ca-

Man has a right to exert an influence and the responsibility to be influenced.

Markku Graae,
Skills Academy Ltd

With support from other people, we can quickly increase the benefits provided by ICT through identifying our own level of expertise and challenges in proportion to the capacity and opportunities offered by our PC hardware and software. One must take determined steps, even if they are small, to reach one's own optimum level.

Markku Markkula, MP

pacity to learn, to such a degree that it will enable us to change our own ideas and open up new views. In an information society, a learning-oriented individual is an explorer who actively seeks new incentives and opportunities to realise his or her ambitions, to create new knowledge and act in co-operation with others. He or she has a passion to learn.

Information which fails to take effect, or which is not passed on to exert an influence, is one of the factors causing information overload in knowledge work. We are exposed to such a deluge of information, both in the form of paper and electronically, that many people are simply not capable of mastering the situation. In the future, the methods and tools of information prioritisation and knowledge management will become increasingly important development targets. The development of personal work methods could ensure total control of the related tools and their updates on a continual basis. Do we really know how much time we could save by learning to exploit, even relatively efficiently, the resources provided by our personal computers in the form of various software packages and models? Determined efforts to achieve one's own optimum level (in proportion to the learning time, other resources, one's own work and assignments) form the basic tool to accomplish results.

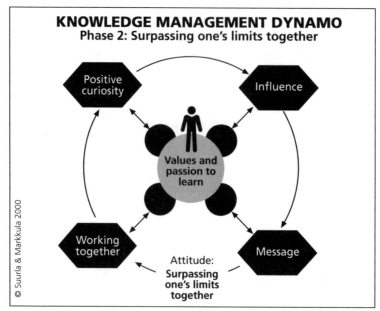

Picture 22: KM Dynamo, phase 2. Surpassing one's limits together

Phase two is used to describe the fostering of values as the capacity and ability of an individual, with the passion for learning, to surpass his or her personal limits and learn to work with other people. We can use positive questioning to discover new things and perceive opportunities instead of threats. This makes exerting influence easier and more natural. If we can participate and have the energy to be active we will find it easier to produce something personal to say, something that is needed in networking, for example.

It is the individual's personal responsibility as a lifelong learner that is emphasised in the information society. From the point of view of the community and society, this will have both positive and negative effects. A strong emphasis on individuality with entirely new types of opportunities for success are calling for a substantial increase in ethical thinking, due to the fact that the said success cannot be shared by all people. Those who are not capable of managing their learning process or maintaining their own professional expertise must be provided with external support. Society cannot be the only support provider in an information society. Instead, the communities and the individuals must take a fair share of this responsibility alike.

This means that learning cannot remain just an unconditional necessity—it must be adapted into becoming a resource that generates new strength and makes knowledge effective and sensible. Knowledge can only be effective if it is meaningful.

Trust and positive questioning

Trust should appear as the people's capability of positive questioning and their ability to jointly process the ideas and views produced. Combining other people's views with one's own and promoting them, advances the spirit of innovation. An atmosphere of trust will enable the handling of all matters, even the most difficult ones. However, even if the dissemination of knowledge is facilitated by electronic aids, the most significant resource will continue to be the individual with his or her personal knowledge processing capacity. People are in a position to make knowledge effective, furthermore they have the responsibility to use all means available to ensure that the knowledge they disseminate is reliable. Positive questioning, drafting ideas together, and creating new knowledge are efforts for which ample time, space and conditions must be reserved.

> Knowledge-quality management, information security and ethics are intertwined. The items of information and knowledge that you pass on must be well-prepared and disseminated in an easy-to-grasp fashion to recipients.
> **Riitta Korhonen, MP**

According to knowledge management theories, trust and openness are the indispensable prerequisites for knowledge to be passed on, take effect and generate new knowledge. Concealing knowledge is a tool for domination and contrary to the knowledge management ideology. For the purpose of creating new knowledge together, wisdom is power. What does this mean in practice to working communities?

Openness and influence

In this context, openness is used with special reference to openness in work methods and work processes. An ideal solution would be to build such a work culture with the preparatory processes for various matters being open to such a degree that all relevant parties could interact continually at the various stages of the process. This is extremely important, in parliamentary work in particular.

> A smoothly functioning administrative system is a national success factor. For administration to be competitive in practice, electronic communication is a must, in addition shortening the reaction times in various functions, achieving lean central government, and emphasising the responsibility of local authority.
>
> **Paavo Lipponen, Prime Minister of Finland**

Co-operation between Parliament and the various ministries, in preparatory legislative work, for example, has come up frequently during this project. The MPs participating in the steering group emphasised the need to influence the content of legislative proposals during the preparatory process, and not delaying it until the bills' parliamentary debate. In an era of electronic communication media, increasing openness would be an easy matter. Unbending attitudes, incompatible software packages, etc., constitute impediments for these arrangements. Impediments to openness consist of a wide variety of factors. Quite frequently, power and work routines are the issue.[82]

> In electronic law-drafting, it would be natural to provide access to the matters at hand to all members of the preparatory unit who have a contribution to make to the project in question. Instead of being summoned formally once a week to a rigid meeting in a conference room and having to make and listen to mediocre, relatively badly prepared statements, the participants could interact and communicate on a continual basis. This would make administration essentially more transparent.
>
> **Klaus Frösén, Ministerial Counsellor, the Ministry of the Environment**

As early as 1979, the Club of Rome emphasised the role of participation as the precondition for all responsible learning in its report "No Limits to Learning". Participation not only refers to presence or mere discussion of matters but also to practical deeds and taking an evaluating stand in common affairs. There is no real influence without participation.

Knowledge work provides a wide range of opportunities for participation and influence through the Internet, even if the existing electronic working environments must be developed further to make this possible. What is significant from the point of view of knowledge management is the people's own active role as debate instigators and progenitors of interaction. Openness also refers to ethical transparency that can be realised more effectively when matters can be discussed at all phases of the process.

During the brief period of its independence, Finland never was "the Promised Land of Discussion" but rather the opposite. One may say that public debate still is extremely difficult in Finland. Nevertheless, the future is not dictated by the past, which means that, in the current situation, it is also up to the present generations to make a choice. The opportunities provided by ICT could be exploited to create a versatility of interactive networks between people and information systems, thus providing a forum for comprehensive discussion—if so required. Value-based choices will inevitably be involved in this issue, among others.

Irma Levomäki, Researcher,
Helsinki University, Department of social and moral philosophy

Sharing and one's personal message

Sharing is the unconditional prerequisite for networking. Sharing invariably calls for something valuable from the recipient's viewpoint—a message. There are two things to learn—how to share, and how to create something to say. Naturally, each knowledge worker has a network of his or her own where they operate actively. However, there is a continual need to expand one's personal network, and to create new ones. Networking is not confined to meeting people. It also means virtual communication. As a goal-oriented activity, networking includes the sharing and diffusion of messages, mutual help and dissemination of knowledge.

How can one act efficiently in a network in terms of knowledge management? A knowledge worker receives an abundance of information of various types, of which he or she can utilise only a fraction. A net-

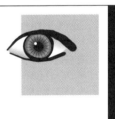

From time to time, check when you personally met people from your intimate network and spent more than two hours with them on a free-form basis. If it was more than three months ago, arrange such a meeting. (Skyrme 1999.)

work can be used to make material and knowledge accessible to all participants, some of whom may benefit from it and put the knowledge in question to a wider use. The principle of mutual help and sharing has been identified as a major resource in knowledge management. In addition to time, this will require above all bothering to act on it, plus a vision of the type of knowledge to be shared to each network and to the select individuals currently present in the network in question. There is too much knowledge, so a message must be included in the communication. In addition, one must learn to assess the type of knowledge the network members need.

Doing and learning together

The key skill in joint knowledge management activities, learning together and doing things together, lies in listening to and appreciating other people's views and opinions. Just doing a number of things together will not be enough; instead, efforts should be made to produce a forum of interaction that also contributes to the creation of new knowledge. For this to be possible, people must learn to listen to one another, hear new messages and meanings, and appreciate one another's capabilities and expertise.

The ways and means of a work place to cope with "the global pack of wolves" are crystallised as doing together, increasing the reliance capital and improving learning together. We must generate a process where everyone wins, in other words, to achieve outstanding business profitability on the global scale and to improve the personnel's well-being and opportunities for participation. This will also enable more efficient use of economic rewards through result-based salaries and wages. As a result, we will also be able to care for the less fortunate and preserve the essential elements of our Nordic welfare state.

Veikko Teikari, Professor, Helsinki University of Technology

Hearing requires the preparedness to expand one's own viewpoints, to tolerate different types of thinking, and a willingness to change one's ideas. If prevailing, various and contradictory views cannot be expressed, creativity will cease and no new ideas will emerge. However, there must be a possibility to convert ideas into tangible innovations, which in turn necessitates doing things together, plus the adoption of other people's thoughts and tacit knowledge.

Hearing always occurs on other people's conditions. One must be humane and close to others.
Riitta Korhonen, MP

Am I listening to you?
I am not listening to you when:

- I do not care for you.
- I say I understand before I know you well.
- I have an answer for your problem before you have finished telling me what your problem is.
- I cut you off before you have finished speaking.
- I finish your sentence for you.
- I am critical of your grammar, vocabulary or accent.
- I am dying to tell you something.
- I tell you about my experiences, making yours seem unimportant.
- I am really communicating with someone else in the room.
- I refuse your thanks saying that I have not really done anything.

I am listening to you when:

- I come quietly into your private world and let you be you.
- I really try to understand you even if you are not making much sense.
- I grasp your point of view even when it is against my own convictions.
- I realise that the time you give to me is very important.
- I allow you the dignity of making your own decisions even though I may think they are wrong.
- I do not take your problem from you, but allow you to deal with it in your own way.
- I hold back my desire to give you good advice.
- I give you room to discover for yourself what is really going on.
- I accept your gratitude by telling you how good it is to know I have been helpful.

(Wickens 1999.)

Thanks to efficient information diffusion and knowledge dissemination, recipients (individuals, communities or society) can change their ideas and learn more. However, the knowledge provider must also learn new things from the recipient on a continual basis, for the project's products and services to develop, for example. This involves not only interaction but also learning together in a profound sense. In terms of its results, interaction may be restricted to communication between just two or at most a few people, taking turns exerting an influence. However, even if some influence could be perceived in their work, it is possible that each of them is acting alone.

To enable genuine joint activities and a shared creative process, changes must take place during interaction in such a manner that they change the reality where the people in question work and live their lives. Building together will change the thinking and deeds of all parties involved while the process is in progress (see Figure 23). This brings the participants into a continual dialogue with other people, work and reality where action takes place through learning and learning through action.[83] A dialogue differs from ordinary conversation, for example, in that in dialogue, all parties learn new things from one another and create new knowledge together.

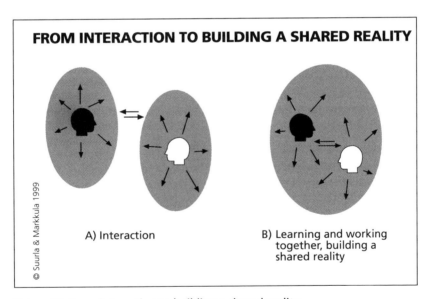

Picture 23: From interaction to building a shared reality

As such, knowledge has always been a central issue in various cultures and societies. In this respect, all historical societies have been "information societies". Without a quantitative increase of knowledge, progress to an industrial society would have been impossible. At the current stage of development, however, the role of information and knowledge is increasingly highlighted, compared to previous historical development.[84]

A similar statement can be made with regard to values. As such, the importance of values is nothing new. The permanent change instigated by the advent of an information society, with sustaining learning requirements also means a major threat to the people. Increasing insecurity will lead to increasing exhaustion and discomfort. If a person experiences future challenges as something insurmountable, his or her life will be permanently insecure. When externally provided security decreases, one must be personally capable of adapting quickly. Creativity helps one perceive new opportunities and awareness of one's own values provides increasing self-confidence and motivation to make new efforts. When undergoing a process of drastic change, a person's permanent security must be based on strong values and creativity.

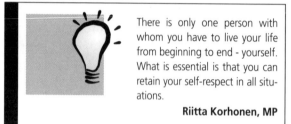

There is only one person with whom you have to live your life from beginning to end - yourself. What is essential is that you can retain your self-respect in all situations.

Riitta Korhonen, MP

A report by the Committee for the Future (1998) mentions that the 20th century is the century of human rights. Towards the end of the 20th century, human responsibilities are becoming a theme of discussion. The central themes in ethical instructions and various proclamations include humanity, non-violence, respect of life, justice and solidarity, truthfulness and tolerance, mutual respect and partnership. (TuVM 1/1998.)

5.2 Responsible knowledge worker

To be an efficient, innovative and responsible knowledge worker, a person must be capable of exploiting the knowledge and expertise produced by other people, be able to develop his or her core competence on a continual basis, know how to operate in networks, master ICT, and be able to build such a space where he or she can co-operate with others. On this level, the challenge is encountered in changing the work methods towards procedural thinking, in the deliberate combination of various technological tools and methods, and in continuous development of one's own work methods, and in developing new ones.

Experts and the process of creation

The basic knowledge management material consists of the knowledge capital that is invested in people.

In addition to this investment, however, the question is how to benefit from the investment-contained knowledge capital with maximum efficiency and how to create new knowledge. The 'experts' term is used here to describe an organisation's or a community's human resources, which must be sufficient to provide an adequate amount of time to be consumed. The continual decreasing of resources will inevitably lead to a situation where no time can be spared for creative work. This is the major paradox encountered in knowledge work. The fact that creativity re-

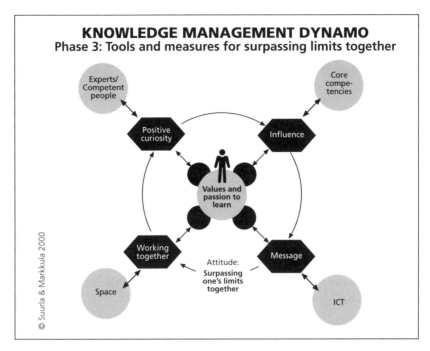

Picture 24: KM Dynamo, phase 3. Tools and steps to carry out in the process of change

quires time is being ignored, along with the people's need to interact without the confines of profit-based objectives. The creative process is an inherent element of knowledge work and we must find ways to develop it through deliberate measures.

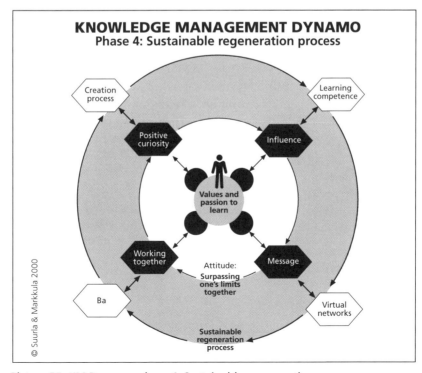

Picture 25: KM Dynamo, phase 4. Sustainable regeneration process.

Core competencies and learning competence

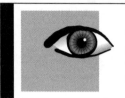

The continual reduction in resources will inevitably lead to a situation where no time can be spared for creative work.

A competence is defined as expert-level capability and skills requiring the following components: explicit and explanatory factual knowledge, skills (know how), experience (tacit knowledge), basic values and internalisation of the working community's principles, plus membership and capability of action in social networks[85] Here, an individual's core competence refers to a number of select expertise areas that are based on his or her own value-related choices and vocational excellence. The capability of participation and exerting an influence is based on openness, among other factors. For participation to be effective it must take place within the realm of one's core competence, otherwise one will fail to provide it with a message, or find the time, will, incentive, or courage to do it. Conversely, it is only in the area of a person's core competence where he or she can realise that more effective personal participation will require personal recognition of openness as a value, plus the realisation of its ethical implications.

In the future, the concept of intellectual capital will include the idea that each employee is his or her own employer and personally responsible for the development of his or her own expertise.

**Esko Kilpi,
Management Consultant,
Sedecon Consulting Ltd**

We use the concept of a learning competence to emphasise that the core competencies, or main areas of expertise, must be updated and developed on a continual basis for knowledge workers to retain their competitiveness in the labour market. It is the process of development that brings expertise to life and makes it challenging.

Furthermore, competence development involves the care for social and intellectual capital—not professional development alone. Connections to work processes, work community ethics and other people are included in this issue.

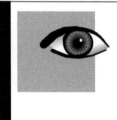

Where some knowledge workers are enjoying the benefits of short-term employment without having to commit themselves for years to a specific work place, others are suffering from its adverse affects. Nurses, cleaners and department store till operators are also entitled to knowledge and the learning of new things. But is a young short-term employee, who is at the brink of exhaustion, really capable of finding the time and space for his or her personal innovativeness while simultaneously having to fill the standards of a perfectly qualified employee in expectation of a subsequent employment period?

Susanna Huovinen, MP

ICT and virtual networks

In an information society, mastery of the information and communication technologies (ICT) is a must. This does not only refer to ICT as such, but also to personal communication and interaction skills, as has been repeatedly stated above.

Compatible hardware and data support are becoming increasingly important, due to the fact that incompatible hardware and lack of data support will cause a waste of time, money and resources. For example, storing information on the PC hard disk and in the e-mail pro-

An individual must receive support to clarify his or her personal aptitude and future vision. To complement our technological expertise, we need a unit that specialises in the study of man's motivation structure and the provision of appropriate encouragement and incentives.
Kyösti Karjula, MP

gram for easy retrieval as required, is a surprisingly difficult task. Each knowledge worker should have the type of hardware and software that is best suited for his or her requirements, which does not mean the most expensive models on the market.

Information systems management includes compatibility between various technical devices and software packages installed in various environments, plus a guarantee for information storage and availability and ease of use. The organisation's hardware upgrade policy is also highly relevant. Holistic planning is very important since the progress of a specific issue is all too often cut short by technical details in knowledge work. Virtual networks will fail to function if the people involved are not familiar with the technology. E-mail is but one of the many tools of a knowledge worker. He or she must also be able to use various virtual learning environments and joint workspaces. Both electronic systems and operating skills of their users must be continually developed and updated. Many new developments are simply resisted because people cannot use a specific program or never find the time to learn how to use it. Information system specialists must take the users into account, even when planning the implementation and installation of various software packages. Solving this problem is imperative. This calls for support from information system specialists and, frequently, continuous co-operation between both ICT professionals and the people who use the ICT-facilities provided. Small problems often cause major drawbacks. Interaction and the drafting of ideas together could help in these matters also.

One of the challenges we are facing in the Ministry of the Environment is to develop interaction. Co-operation in teams would be good practice for our activities. A precondition for this is that the managerial level can set objectives for each team and motivate people to work together to achieve the goals defined.
Klaus Frösén, Ministerial Counsellor, the Ministry of the Environment

Space and Ba

Here, space is used to refer to a point in time, a location and culture between people, which advances joint activities and joint learning. It has been observed that, from the point of view of knowledge dissemination and diffusion of new ideas, open workspaces are more favourable than closed, isolated office rooms. The Ba thinking will enhance networking and the exchange of ideas between people. We must work in co-operation with various groups of professionals in workspace planning, since each party has something new to learn. As open space is not well-suited to each and every type of work, various alternatives must be created and used flexibly at various stages of work.

MPs have experience of using the Parliament Café as significant space of the Ba type. This is a place to meet colleagues and people from various walks of life. Improving the functionality of Ba-spaces is a common cause for all parties. In addition to the one mentioned above, more space of the Ba type should be established within the parliamentary premises. Furthermore, new methods of work could be developed as well.

Developing the methods used in joint activities and systematising the meetings of experts from various fields would increase the possibilities of benefiting directly from Ba-type activities.

 Ba is a multi-dimensional forum of activities and an environment with constantly changing boundaries where people share, create and exploit knowledge together. This takes place both in the people's thinking (sharing ideas) and in their action (doing together). The creation of knowledge calls for an encouraging environment and frame of reference due to the fact that the context provides the knowledge with meaning. To be able to interpret knowledge and create meaning, man needs a social, cultural and historical reference frame. (Nonaka & Toyama & Konno 2000.)

Compartmentalising and confining activities to one's own field is common in the world of science, in organisational activities and among the specialists in various industries. In an information society, however, we are increasingly challenged to participate in joint efforts, which means that people will have to learn to understand one another's special terminology and modes of expression, to a certain degree, at least. The best way to learn this is to learn it straight from the specialist. For this to succeed, all the parties involved must strive for a sufficient clarity of communication that will make learning possible. This calls for a humble attitude.

In their knowledge management research, Nonaka, Toyama and Konno emphasise the fact that both the researchers and the business and organisation management are aware of how important knowledge management is and take it as one the crucial success factors in an information society. Nevertheless, they speak rather about information management than knowledge management. According to Nonaka et al., the reason is that we lack the understanding of what knowledge, and the knowledge creation process ultimately contains. For example, as the western leadership tradition suggests, an organisation is, to an excessive extent, seen as a machine that receives information and processes it using problem-solving methods in accordance with the objective defined. A static and passive organisation of this type is never capable of a dynamic knowledge creation process.

Instead of discussing its internal problems, an organisation should reshape its work culture towards the emphasis of joint knowledge creation and interactive processes. The organisation should also interact with the environment so as to be able to influence both the environment and its own activities within the knowledge creation process. To understand a dynamic process of this type, calls for a new type of research into organisations' leadership, how organisations interact with their environment, and how their personnel interact with one another. According to Nonaka et al., the central issue in the knowledge creation process is dialectical thinking, which surpasses boundaries and combines contradictory aspects, such as order and chaos, micro and macro levels, entities and their parts, mind and body, explicit and tacit knowledge, deduction and induction, creativity and control.[86]

Consider This!

Consider the various ways to improve information distribution, and how to ensure ideas flourish in your organisation. How do you reward and encourage people? What do you criticise them for? What does feedback mean to you personally?

If you have answered like most people, you will find the left-hand column easier to fill than the right-hand one. However, try to fill them both.

Various ways to enhance information distribution and knowledge dissemination within you team.

STICKS   CARROTS

_____   _____

_____   _____

_____   _____

_____   _____

_____   _____

Figure 26. Work method, an example (Bukowitz & Williams 1999).

Competition

The Committee for the Future's TA Steering Group spent 10 days in the U.S.A investigating the local information society in Boston, Washington D.C. and Silicon Valley, California. The major difference between the U.S.A. and Europe, including Finland, is, perhaps, of the intellectual kind. Intellectual competition was distinctly perceived everywhere. Competition was seen as something positive, contrary to Finland where it is most often interpreted as a negative phenomenon, or, at least, as a questionable method of action. Below are a few sentences that we heard during the trip, which reflect the meaning of this new type of competition and ambition. We heard people speak as follows:

"When my little daughter was learning Spanish, a new language, she was proud, and the whole family was proud of her. Next she might take up Japanese, for example. As you know, we American get along with English, of course, but to manage in a new, global world, it is wise to invest in the future."

"It is great that one of the 10 new start-up businesses survived and that eight of those who went bankrupt started a new enterprise immediately."

"How do we start student exchanges from Stanford University (the same applies all the universities we visited, including the MIT, Berkeley and Harvard) to Finland? Contracts, orders from the top, or any kind of attractions will probably not help. Students and teachers are extremely ambitious. They want the best— the best teaching in particular. A good teacher attracts the best students, and the best students will do everything in their power to be tutored by the best teacher. Personal commitment, access to the intellectual atmosphere of a guru is an advantage that cannot be measured in money."

"I am not looking for money. I already have a good idea and the support of local investors (business angels) from Oulu, Finland. What I need is new knowledge and people with guts to work for me", was the answer we got from a young Finn, aged about 25, when asked whether he was looking for financial support in Silicon Valley.

"Previously, our students (Stanford, Berkeley, Harvard, MIT) used to seek employment in large, secure businesses, banks, insurance companies and government agencies, but now they want to set up a business of their own: Once they get it up and running, they are thirsty to establish another, either alone or with a team of like-minded people."

Paula Tiihonen, Committee Counsellor, the Committee for the Future

5.3 Systematic knowledge management development

The Knowledge Management Dynamo provides the means to create an illustrative entity of steps to take for the purpose of developing knowledge management. The model can be used to examine one's own operating environment to see which components function appropriately and where improvement is required. The elements combine into a systematic entity, the components of which typically renew themselves on a continual basis. The regeneration process must be of a type that it invariably affects the next element.

For example, when providing time for a creative process, learning new things must be involved in the process. Effective time management calls for changes to be made in the virtual environment, for example, providing access to new reserves of knowledge, or a new working environment where people from the organisation and various external sectors can work together. This will, in turn, generate new needs for activities of the Ba-type. For a new virtual working environment to function in practice, joint meetings are to be used to commit the people involved, allowing them to express questions on the new issue at hand, to exchange experiences, draft ideas together, learn from each other and create new meanings and needs for joint activities. Consequently, this will enhance the growth of the people's common knowledge capital, etc. The continually expanding spiral, which Nonaka introduced, is a desirable development in this connection.

In addition, activities must be continually inspired from outside the community itself, for the KM Dynamo to be continually capable of providing new knowledge and experience. The information and communication technologies provide new opportunities and challenges on a continual basis. Staying at the leading edge of development is a must. Science and art also provide new incentives and ideas. One must be able to adopt new knowledge and skills, and to share them with other experts. We must learn how to share tacit knowledge and to exploit networks comprehensively.

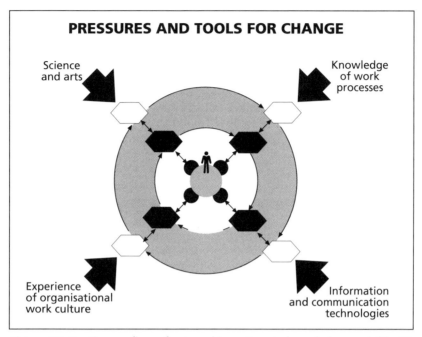

Picture 27: Continuous flow of external incentives in knowledge work (the TA Steering Group).

Interaction must be extensive and it must also cover the contacts between various communities.   This is of special importance in relation to the work of MPs and state administration. The more widely we can exploit the knowledge and experience of our entire society, with increasing citizen participation in common issues, the better are the possibilities for the information society to function. The required technology for extensive interaction already exists; the next question is how to make the technology serve people, and how to make people utilise the opportunities available.

In the U.S.A., development towards the information society is seen clearly in the country's top universities. All the universities visited had major projects in progress to develop Internet-based learning. On the one hand, efforts were being made to develop more efficient teaching materials (all lectures were available as videos through the Internet), and, on the other hand, to make the entire process of study more flexible and more versatile. Distance learning as part-time study during employment is also seen as a major trend for the future in universities. Even now, Berkley University has some 32,000 full-time resident students, plus another 65,000 distance learners in the Extension Programme who complete their lectures, practical exercises and examinations via the Internet.
Kimmo Halme, Chief Planning Officer, Ministry of Trade and Industry

Increasing opportunities are emerging through the development of information networks and software packages for systematic knowledge management development. The global source of knowledge is available at work places and educational establishments—at any place where there is a computer with an Internet connection. The deployment of Web-based work methods with the development of group-specific methods will increase the teams' and communities' results, especially in cases where the people are mobile and working permanently in a joint physical space is not possible or expedient. Doing things together is also learning together. Exploitation of virtual networks and new user-friendly software packages will change people's work and study habits significantly in the foreseeable future.

The TA Steering Group members familiarised themselves with the current eBusiness and eLearning development efforts in progress in the USA. The impression was that the eLearning sector will rapidly develop into a major business in the global market. According to several expert sectors, the eLearning business is currently undergoing a similar stage, with an identical potential for growth, as the telecommunication cluster was 10 years ago. International comparisons indicate that Finnish people are willing and eager to exploit the opportunities provided by technological development. Finland is a country with considerable development efforts in progress. The virtual university project, several ICT projects launched within the national education system, plus a national content production project are indisputably producing good results.

Finnish society, educational establishments, work places and other communities have excellent opportunities to develop and become cutting edge operators in the field of eLearning and related new practices in the global market. What is required in the present situation is to have the capability and courage to make sufficient investments in order to create Finnish-made successful products and services and supply them to the global market.

5.4 Proposals to develop the Finnish Parliament's knowledge management activities

This chapter is based on the discussions of the TA Steering Group. It includes ideas, as well as detailed proposals, about the Parliament's knowledge management development needs. The analysis is based on using the Knowledge Management Dynamo and the knowledge management principles, which were described above. Once a value-based work process has been launched to progress systematically with the aid of the KM Dynamo, it will generate new ideas and development proposals on a continual basis.

Trust—positive speculation—creative process

Continuous haste is seen as a major problem in parliamentary work. This is a common problem in all other work cultures in our society. The KM Dynamo emphasises awareness of the basic philosophy, to allow people to develop appropriate means for problem solving. Haste cannot be eliminated through technological development alone. The most attention must be paid to what people want to have instead of haste. Mere extra time will not solve the problem. We must become aware of how we actually want to develop our activities. A future-oriented person who applies knowledge cre-

Innovativeness generates innovativeness - but only in a trustworthy and trusting growth environment.
Riitta Korhonen, MP

atively should replace a busy individual on the brink of exhaustion. One must be able to use one's personal knowledge toolbox to organise new knowledge in such a fashion that it can be exploited and consolidated for dissemination and distribution to others. The individual's personal mission and his or her conscious values, which are applicable in practice, will support activities of this type.

Innovativeness and promotion of creativity are significant motivators that make work more rational. However, creativity requires time for positive speculation and an atmosphere of trust where ideas can be shared without restrictions. The central role of creative thinking and the development of creativity are essential elements in the elimination of haste. During the course of our project, we have emphasised the importance of jointly produced ideas and creative input. Creative joint activities not only consume time but also generate new energy.

Proposals to develop activities

- Expert aid should be developed in such a manner that the experts involved would not only present brief statements from their papers but would co-operate with MPs and would be engaged in creative dialogue with them. Experts can also be heard in video conferences with better possibilities to use illustrative material, also avoiding time-consuming travel. These occasions must be developed in a direction that generates mutual appreciation between MPs and experts, thus enabling knowledge to be shared and ideas to be jointly generated.

- The work of an MP includes a large number of meetings. It is considered important that the meeting practices be developed in a way that makes information more effective. A precondition for this is that part of the meeting procedure be replaced by participation through increasing use of joint activities, brainstorming and dialogue.

- A specific portion of each MP's work should consist of interaction with the nation's various sectors (teachers, information visits to schools, collaboration with special groups, etc.). Activities of this type can be developed and existing experiences shared through various discussion forums, for example.

Openness—influence—developing competence

Several MPs participating in the Steering Group have emphasised the importance of developing openness in the parliamentary work methods. Openness is emphasised, for example, in interaction between MPs, in that between citizens and MPs, and in preliminary legislative work between government officials. The MPs' expertise could be exploited more efficiently at an earlier stage while various bills are being prepared. In addition, co-operation could be used to develop the participants' innovativeness. Development of the prevailing debate culture and the means of influence are inherent components of continual development in the MPs' core competence areas. This development must be plan-based and goal-directed.

Proposals to develop activities

- Raising the MPs' expertise level and emphasising their personal mission. Each MP should produce his or her personal development plan in the form of a work chart, for example, with continuous updates (see Chapter 6). Concrete partial learning targets would be scheduled in a calendar with ample time reserved for learning. The fact that each MP has a personal mission will enable the construction of a personally significant expertise profile. Profiling will highlight the elements of expertise, instead of everyone trying to master everything.

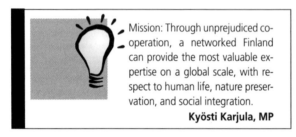

Mission: Through unprejudiced co-operation, a networked Finland can provide the most valuable expertise on a global scale, with respect to human life, nature preservation, and social integration.
Kyösti Karjula, MP

- Study opportunities can be increased, for example, by developing eLearning services, learning environments and study units on various themes for use by MPs on the Internet. Electronic learning environments will also facilitate co-operation with experts.

- Co-operation between MPs and the Ministries should be developed through improving joint activities during the bill drafting process. MPs must participate in the handling of all essential questions before the bills are submitted to Parliament. The regulations of public administration emphasise an open preparatory process where the views of various sectors and parties, for example, are clarified and exploited during the bill drafting stage. Web-based work methods can also be used to include civic organisations, experts in the field, and private citizens who have practical experience in the matters at hand.

- The bills submitted to Parliament should be presented in a more illustrative fashion (for example using presenter-made OHP transparencies and other material, not by the mere reading aloud from a paper). This calls for the acquisition of appropriate audiovisual equipment for the conference rooms.

- Developing a quality assurance system for legislative work to allow for the consideration of regional differences in the laws being passed. (Cf. the problems of the Helsinki region versus the rest of Finland.)

- To ensure adequate resources for expert group activities within the Parliament's small group budget, hobby club and specific expert panel activities should be budgeted separately. Both functions are important but the hobby clubs' resource requirement must not engulf the finances reserved for expert group work and vice versa.

Sharing—message —virtual networks

To be able to operate efficiently in various networks, one must have a message to communicate. This will be increasingly emphasised when people want to participate actively in virtual network activities and develop eLearning environments. At present, MPs use the Internet, mobile phones and e-mail for virtual networking. The Parliament is continuously developing its electronic communication management methods and tools (see Chapter 6). An MP's knowledge toolbox is also updated and developed on a continual basis, like the various components of the KM Dynamo.

Parliamentary work is versatile and presupposes prompt reactivity. Like any other modern professionals, MPs also need pertinent knowledge management tools and aids. International work and related needs for comparison (Finland versus other countries) have generated new pressures for knowledge management. The possibilities to benefit more efficiently from knowledge material through state-of-the-art technology have increased with the growing number of assistant personnel. This means that the envisioned knowledge toolbox would only function efficiently through co-operation between the MP and his or her personal assistant, due to the tight parliamentary work schedule.

Proposals to develop activities

Regarding the items of knowledge and ICT solutions, an MP's knowledge toolbox would contain the following entities:

- Easy-to-use links to existing files that are organised per subject matter

- Automatic access to updated key numbers, messages, novelty hints, etc.

- Links to central think tanks and public authorities providing analytic and pre-processed knowledge that the MP in question has selected for monitoring

- Service pages where various statistics are provided with context. Thus, one could get an overall picture of the issue at hand from an example.

- Information service organised per subject matter for use by Parliamentary Committees, with MPs participating in the update procedure. This information service would provide, for example, OHP transparency sets of current interest, including those produced by MPs. All MPs would have access to these transparency sets for use in their own presentations, for example. The information service would include a retrieval system based on topic division.

- Easy-to-use links to the following existing databases, as required, to enable active interaction, with a possibility to edit information and knowledge for personal needs (statistical and other files):
  - Statistics Finland
  - Files pertaining to the economy / Bank of Finland, Ministry of Finance, Government Institute for Economic Research, Employers' Confederation of Service Industries in Finland, Finnish National Fund for Research and Development, Research Institute of the Finnish Economy, Technical Research Centre of Finland, Academy of Finland, Central Organisation of Finnish Trade Unions, Confederation of Finnish Industry and Employers
  - National Research and Development Centre for Welfare and Health (STAKES), and other units that produce societal knowledge
  - OECD, EU, UN, World Bank, ILO
  - Political research institutes
  - Information services and links provided by libraries
  - Archives of newspapers and journals

The Internet can help us build confidence between citizens and MPs without the media interfering and interpreting the messages being exchanged.
Irina Krohn, MP

- Internet pages and ready-made activity packages to enable debate initiated by individuals, either alone or together with a specific group, concerning political questions, within selected discussion groups or interest groups, or nationwide (cf. A 60-minute Internet-discussion with 22 young people (and other citizens) on critical points in the future of work, organised by the Committee for the Future on 20th September, 2000). Test ballots would also be easy to arrange.

- To be able to exploit knowledge effectively without a deluge of information, we must produce service packages of various levels for the various types of MPs. The packages would vary with regard to their content, technology applied and operating features available. Some are satisfied to receive just the article titles or summaries and newsletters on a regular basis on specific, clearly defined topics. Some only need domestic information. Others require comprehensive international material and even want to personally edit the complex spreadsheets or indicators they receive. One MP only wants a few ideas on current topics as a basis for a good, old-fashioned incendiary speech, while another may wish to illuminate the entire historical development to the audience on his or her speech tour with accurate statistical details from a portable PC.

- The toolbox should contain a number of entities in the form of books, pictures, hard copies and electronic files. All MPs would not have to be able to master everything, provided that information and knowledge can be effectively distributed within their own parliamentary group or the committee involved. This will allow the specialisation and division of labour in knowledge management. What is essential is to build a parliamentary knowledge management system reserved for the exclusive use of in-house personnel. The system-contained items would be updated automatically; thus providing access to up-to-date information at all times in the form of tables and graphs, both on paper and as transparencies.

- In the current situation, one cannot accept the premise that each and everyone should personally acquire the required information or seek and select something suitable from among the 100 tables provided by the Statistics Finland, for example. Furthermore, mere passive links or Web site references are also insufficient. Service is required in the form of co-operation between users and information system specialists. An example of existing, functional databases are the article file archives of major news-printing houses that serve journalists in their work. The topics, writers, in-depth background information and links are found, even from long-term periods, with the aid of user-friendly search engines. The Parliament's personal librarian service could also be made more effective.

- Software compatibility and hardware compatibility have always caused problems, which will probably recur in the future since organisations, and people, progress at different speeds when adopting new technology. Parliament's exprience is quite comprehensive in this regard. For example, the parliamentary IT systems have mainly used Corel software applications while the outside world has been using Microsoft software. However, excellent support services, including automatic software compilers, have provided significant assistance. Nevertheless, interoperability will continue to be a major challenge.

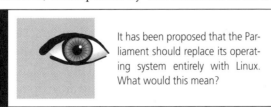

It has been proposed that the Parliament should replace its operating system entirely with Linux. What would this mean?

An additional objective of this knowledge toolbox is to pick "pearls" for MPs to use, or, at least, to create real possibilities of finding them. Since knowledge acquisition costs money, it would be advisable to establish a specific, joint information service system for all the MPs and their assistants. Time is money, even in knowledge acquisition. However, the main issue is to improve the quality of parliamentary work by providing MPs with more efficient access to information and knowledge through existing technologies.

> Access to data, information and knowledge should not be restricted to the use of desktop computers in Finland, the leading country in the mobile technology market. An MP aptly described a typical knowledge management situation of his: "I daily rush from one meeting to another, type short messages on my tiny mobile phone and attend to many errands between the meetings. If I only had a decent Communicator at my disposal, with ample space for more text, and an Internet connection with e-mail, I could deal with those on the spot and would not have to put off everything until the late hours to look into on my office PC.
>
> What if we launched a pilot project and surveyed our possibilities to enhance the existing efficiency and user friendliness level. Parliament could acquire various mobility boosting devices for trial periods for use by those MPs who are willing to act as guinea pigs."
>
> (Thoughts of a MP during a busy decision period in December 1999.)

Doing things together—learning together—Ba

Joint activities and learning together probably impose the most exacting challenges—all components of the Knowledge Management Dynamo are geared towards meeting them. Ba emphasises a location and space with sufficient opportunities to generate the type of activity leading to the creation of new knowledge. At present, the Parliament Café serves the purpose of knowledge distribution relatively well with various parties and sectors meeting to share information and one another's views. Nevertheless, more space is required for joint creation of new knowledge by several people—both physically and mentally. People must not only be happy within this space but also be aware of and actively take responsibility along with others.

Proposals to develop activities
- Launching a forum for joint learning - Ba. Developing dialogue (learning-oriented discussions) between MPs, public employees, and experts from various sectors through joint learning forums where MPs can also participate as specialists from theirs own fields, in addition to their capacity as societal opinion leaders. The forum meetings would provide material for TV discussions and educational programmes. Concentrating on future-related discussion, for example, on pondering the main trends weak signals of future work could initially launch these forums for joint learning. The forum topics would arise from the MPs' own interests in their line of work. MPs would personally enrol as forum experts.

- Launching knowledge management forums where MPs share the latest knowledge management user experience and learn from each other. These activities can be implemented as per Parliamentary Committee, for example, and in co-operation with the Parliament's information systems management specialists.

The purpose of this assessment project concentrating on technological impacts was to clarify the effects of knowledge management on work and work cultures. During the course of this project, the Steering Group members also concentrated on the Parliament's own knowledge management activities and went considerably deeper than usual.

This Parliament-wide knowledge management development project, which was launched in the autumn of 2000, promoted many views expressed in this report for practical application in parliamentary work (see Chapter 6). People who are enthusiastic about their work easily produce ideas and well-grounded views on how to develop or change the work processes of their own work community. A more difficult task is to personally commit oneself to diligent work to implement one's ideas. To achieve desirable changes, however, is a long and strenuous process. The TA Steering Group hopes that the various parties and sectors involved will have the energy to delve deep into the envisioned policy lines.

Striving towards the vision of a true knowledge society, a society of increasing wisdom, will emphasise the goal-oriented aspects of our debate culture, its increasing openness requirement and its aesthetic transparency. It is impossible to require or presuppose such a culture. It must be internalised through learning. We must develop methods for doing things together in addition to genuine joint activities in our work.

TA Steering Group

6. Applying knowledge management principles to parliamentary work

6.1 Parliamentary knowledge management
Overview

The Parliament's Information Systems and Knowledge Management Project (IS&KM Project) was carried out during the period September 2000–March 2001. The project objective was to produce a joint reference frame and vision for practical knowledge management activities in the Parliament, to consolidate the objectives and means of action, and to provide a basis for further knowledge management development. The project's main results are set out in a reform programme describing the required measures to be taken to develop parliamentary knowledge management. When combined, the Committee for the Future's TA Project on knowledge management and the IS&KM Project formed a comprehensive, multidimensional knowledge management entity that made it possible to consolidate the theoretical frame of reference into a practical action programme.

Due to the extremely exacting and multidimensional nature of knowledge management, the IS&KM Project was launched simultaneously in several fields of action. This was to ensure an adequate perspective to the issue at hand.

Four teams were established: the first to concentrate on solving knowledge management problems in view of parliamentary work planning, the second to focus on internal information services, the third on mapping the needs of MPs and their personal assistants, and the fourth on analysing the possibilities provided by ICT. The teams worked independently but communicated with one another at various forums and reported their progress to the project steering group on a regular basis. During project work, consultants from the TietoEnator company provided support.

In addition to the work of these teams, parliamentary civil servants and MPs were interviewed during the project on their views and experience. The aim was to analyse the assessments of those interviewed regarding parliamentary knowledge management, the competence areas related to daily work, the knowledge requirements and problems, the central changes affecting knowledge management activities in this sphere of multiple responsibilities, and to establish a vision of reliable and efficient knowledge management for the Parliament. Participating in each interview was a TietoEnator consultant and a civil servant involved in the IS&KM Project. The advantage of this method was that parliamentary civil servants and, to a certain extent, even the MPs became better acquainted with one another and the work of their colleagues. This will enhance the sharing and dissemination of knowledge within the organisation, which was also one of the project's immediate objectives.

 This IS&KM Project was based on the following two definitions: Knowledge management consists of systematic development and management of the knowledge, competence and expertise possessed currently by the organisation, and that being acquired by it in future. To be capable of managing knowledge, an organisation must be aware of what knowledge it has, where this knowledge resides, and how to access the knowledge in question. Practical measures within knowledge management are especially knowledge acquisition, processing, storage and distribution. Increasing the effectiveness of knowledge dissemination and sharing is the only way for an organisation to increase remarkably its knowledge.

Knowledge management will enhance the Parliament's routine work efficiency and its capability to react swiftly to societal change as a decision-maker. The central factors causing pressure for change include, for example, the information deluge and its management, and the need for organisations to learn new things increasingly rapidly in a changing action environment. The interviews conducted during the IS&KM Project clearly indicated this view. They also provided the Parliament's line organisation with an excellent opportunity to analyse its own activities.

This chapter describes the Parliament's current knowledge management activities, as well as its knowledge management vision. The teams' and interviewers' observations have been used to convert the target state into a number of development areas to enable further development of the existing, well-functioning services. The primary perspective of this IS&KM Project focused on the Parliamentary Office functions and their development. MPs were involved in this work in the capacity of clients, as a team consisting of a number of MPs and their personal assistants. The Parliamentary Office produces and maintains the services that are required by the Parliament as an organ of government. With regard to knowledge management, the Parliamentary Office is responsible for co-ordinating and maintaining those knowledge acquisition channels and methods that ensure the accessibility and availability of knowledge in accordance with current requirements.

Knowledge management means systematic location, processing, storage and distribution of knowledge, competence and expertise within an organisation. This also refers to the capability to combine and develop existing knowledge so that the creation of new added value is possible. Among other things, this presupposes continual regeneration, learning from one's own and other people's experience, plus an open work culture. The challenge in knowledge management lies in the fact that the most valuable knowledge mainly exists in an undocumented form as tacit knowledge in the minds of the individuals. What is required is the creation of a cultural and technological environment in which all other members of the organisation could exploit this knowledge.

The Parliament's basic information systems, ICT infrastructure and application environment can be exploited in several ways in support of the activities undergoing a process of change. The premise for work was to analyse how new knowledge can be created using existing knowledge to provide the best possible support to parliamentary work and its foreseeable future development.

Concepts and frames of reference

As a concept, the management of knowledge is rather obscure. In his book Älykäs organisaatio (= Intelligent Organisation) Pentti Sydänmaanlakka sets out the following frame of reference to consolidate this concept (see picture 28).

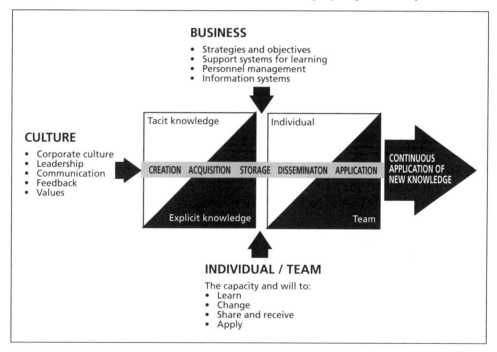

Picture 28. Frame of reference for knowledge management (Sydänmaanlakka, 2000)

The organisation should define what it means by knowledge management. The organisation's strategy and objectives also play an essential role as they can be used to define the types of knowledge that are significant and less significant to its activities. What is also required is support systems for learning, and personnel management, to encourage individuals and teams to create, disseminate and apply new knowledge. It is the organisation culture that provides the framework for knowledge management in its entirety. The organisation's values should also support knowledge distribution and dissemination highlighting knowledge sharing.

Among the significant values that support knowledge sharing, Sydänmaanlakka (2000) mentions lifelong learning, openness and respect for individuals. Other important organisation cultural factors include participatory leadership as well as open and informal communication.

This reference frame can be used for systematic analysis of parliamentary work and parliamentary knowledge management activities. There are several viewpoints, such as the Parliament's tasks, individual MPs and MP groups, submission processes, interest groups, and citizens. The various viewpoints involve different needs for knowledge with various knowledge acquisition methods. For example, the type of knowledge required in committee debates can be obtained by hearing experts, from the Parliament's own information systems, or by turning to in-house information system specialists.

During the interviews, the picture 29 was used as support, to describe the knowledge management dimensions. The purpose of this picture is to indicate that technology is just one of several knowledge management sectors. What is equally important is to develop leadership, processes, an open organisation culture and open organisational activities, strive towards the elimination of boundaries in the spirit of joint objectives, and support learning and networking.

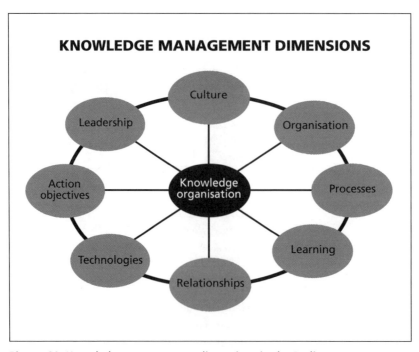

Picture 29. Knowledge management dimensions in the Parliament

6.2 Parliament's IT development phases

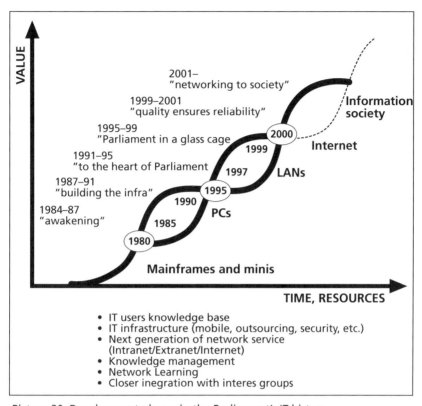

Picture 30. Development phases in the Parliament's IT history

1984—1987 "Time of awakening"

Automation team (ADP team)

Comprehensive study of ADP in legislative work

Process view

Plan to install an IT system to support legislative work

1987—1991 "Building the infrastructure"

First full-time employment for ADP personnel (ADP Manager)

Workstations, cable network, servers

Text processing, e-mail

First joint applications

PCs

ADP unit established

1991—1995 "To the heart of Parliament"

Session hall systems

From ADP to information management

Support to legislative work processes

Management group for IT

1995—1999 "Parliament in a glass cage"
  Intranet/Internet web servers
  Information system for committees
  Structured documents (SGML/XML standard)
  Networking to interest groups (Council of State, citizens)
  Use of interest groups' information systems by Parliament
      (cabinet's decision making system, processing system for EU issues)
  Uniform user interface (WWW browser) to all information systems

1999-2001 "Quality ensures reliability"
  technology dependent parliamentary functions, service reliability
  service quality
  reorganisation of information systems management

2001– "Networking to society"
  internationalisation, EU
  citizens' service provision and interaction
  functional compatibility with central interested parties
      (international partners, etc.)
  ease of use and efficiency
  service provision regardless of time and place
  longevity of systems that support the central functions
  highly reliable ICT structure
  ensuring data system security

Parliament did not embark on the full-scale utilisation of IT until the late 1980s, which was comparatively late. Regardless of the late start, or thanks to it, the progress of parliamentary IT solutions has been quite innovative. Parliament entered the microcomputer era directly, especially that of networked microcomputers. From the very beginning, a process view was adopted for data processing development.

Among other things, this enabled close integration of session hall systems with plenary session work in 1992 and the rapid adoption of Internet-based WWW technology in 1995 when the production databases were connected to WWW servers. A structured document standard (SGML/XML) was adopted for document production, which means that the knowledge produced by Parliament is now available in an easy-to-use form for in-house and external use. In addition, structured legislative documents have enabled the consolidation of the Finnish jurisdiction database.

At present, the Parliament's dependence on ICT is rather extensive. Over the years, parliamentary basic functions and data processing have become integrated to such a degree that it is now difficult, or virtually impossible, to tell them apart. On the one hand, this will provide new opportunities for knowledge management. On the other hand, indulging in extremely sophisticated state-of-the-art ICT solutions may obstruct the sound development of these activities.

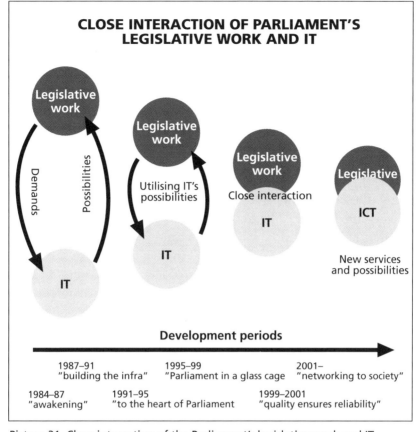

Picture 31. Close interaction of the Parliament's legislative work and IT

An information system management policy regarding the years 2002-2004 was approved in December 2001. On the one hand, the main goals of this period focus on enhancing the use of existing tools, and, on the other hand, on supporting Parliament's external networking activities, towards the citizens and other public administration organisations, among others.

The information systems management policy focuses on the following goals in 2002–2004:

The MPs, their personal assistants and civil servants will be provided with efficient, state-of-the-art ICT tools to support their daily work.

The MPs, their personal assistants and civil servants will have access to up-to-date connections for communicating with various civic organisations and interested parties.

The ICT users' practical skills and know-how will be improved through training in conjunction with the tools replacement, with special attention being paid to personal guidance.

Parliament will establish networking connections with its most important interest groups (the Parliamentary Office, Ministries, the media, libraries, public archives, foreign parliaments, etc.), both technically and regarding the content of services and information provision.

Parliamentary information will be accessible to the general public on a comprehensive basis through the Internet.

Parliament will promote ICT exploitation within its sphere of activities through active participation in national and international development projects, in collaboration between the EU and national parliaments.

The Parliament's Information Systems Management Office will actively monitor information society development, being prepared to respond to emerging needs and requirements.

6.3 Current state of and challenges to development work

According to the Finnish Constitution, power in Finland belongs to the people who are represented by the Parliament in parliamentary sessions. The Parliamentary Office, in turn, is responsible for providing the Parliament with the preconditions to carry out its tasks as an organ of government. In practice, the work of parliamentary civil servants is highly expert-oriented, even with regard to leadership. The organisation units are independent, and even if the organisation does appreciate expertise, the distribution and dissemination of knowledge and expertise has not been adequately appreciated. On the other hand, it is significant that the provision of information, knowledge and services has conventionally been confidential, correct and impartial.

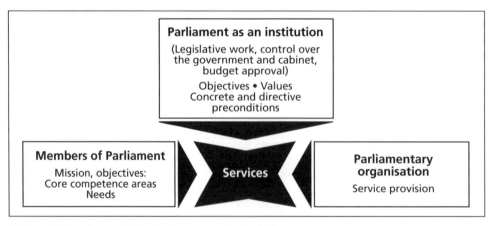

Picture 32. Service provision factors

Parliament employs experts for a wide variety of tasks. This also means that the individuals may personally have quite different knowledge management needs and objectives. With regard to the entity, however, it is possible to distinguish a number of joint objectives, from which concrete directives can be derived for all individuals involved.

As politicians, MPs have knowledge management objectives that differ from those of parliamentary civil servants. The IS&KM Project concentrated on analysing knowledge management needs and objectives, especially from the point of view of the Parliament's constitutional tasks and that of the civil service organisation, which secures the preconditions for parliamentary work and provides the required support services.

Challenges and pressures for change in action environments

As their action environments change, organisations are forced to pay attention to new matters and phenomena. Knowledge management has become one of the greatest challenges encountered by organisations of various types and sizes. This is also due to the parliaments.

Knowledge management is becoming a must for organisations, due to several societal and global phenomena. In a networking world, the volume of manageable knowledge is continually increasing. The primary knowledge management objective is to support and help individuals to cope with the information deluge. There is a need for systematic means and tools to be able to find the correct knowledge at the right time.

Networking will deplete boundaries between organisations and increase individuals' mobility and multicultural communities. Working in such an environment calls for a new way of acting and thinking. In particular, this will change the concept of time—everything should be immediately available—which will make activities increasingly hectic in all sectors.

With exponentially increasing competence and expertise requirements, organisations are expected to be increasingly exacting in monitoring their economy and efficiency, and in achieving improved results, of course. With increasing publicity and the processes becoming more transparent, the development of activities is faced with an additional challenge. Furthermore, a new kind of openness is expected from political activities, which must be taken into account in the preparatory stage and further development.

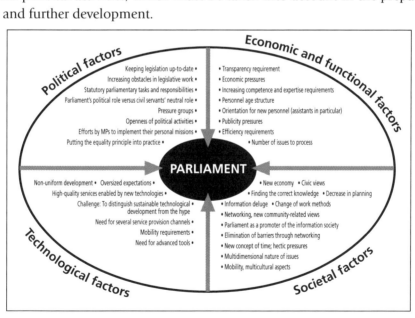

Picture 33. Pressures for change in a parliamentary action environment

Networking, multicultural aspects, and the erosion of boundaries will make legislative work increasingly demanding. Legislators must keep abreast of development, more strictly than ever. Technology has a major role to play in this issue.

People require advanced tools, the possibility to work anywhere, at a time that suits them best in each situation.

New technologies enable high-quality services but, on the other hand, this also increases inequality between people, due to the fact that their capabilities and pre-conditions to exploit new technologies are not all of the same standard. In addition, people have unrealistic, oversized expectations with regard to current technological possibilities, and distinguishing the hype from sustainable technological development is not always easy. Moreover, several sectors are developing their own standards for a joint context, which may cause compatibility problems between various technological solutions.

Observations of the Parliament's current knowledge management status

Parliamentary activities are characterised by a high task performance rate, their partly unpredictable, comprehensive and multidimensional nature, and the mobility of MPs. A significant feature in KM activities is the personal work culture of each MP, his or her individual ICT work method, as well as co-operation and division of labour between MPs and their personal assistants. All of these factors impose a special requirement on the processing and management of knowledge.

Additional characteristic features are caused by the fact that parliamentary elections are held every four years, with the number of new MPs generally being about 25–35%. The practice of personal assistants was introduced four years ago, with each MP deciding whether his or her assistant will work in the Parliament or the MP's electoral district. Turnover has been high among the assistants. Some of the employment relationships have lasted for only a few months, others for several years.

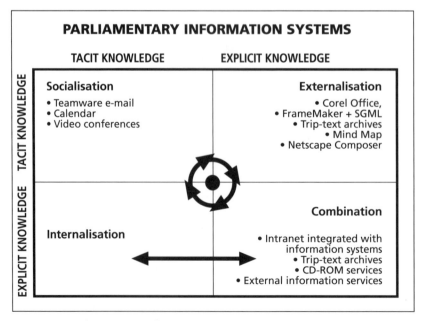

Picture 34. Parliamentary information systems

Parliament has excellent preconditions for its knowledge management development. The parliamentary Intranet (the Fakta system) has established its position as a central distribution channel for in-house information. For the most part, all written material produced by Parliament is accessible through this network, mainly in the form of structured documents. In addition, most of the Parliament's ICT infrastructure is of a high standard and well-functioning.

6.4 Defining the KM target stage

The Parliament's and MPs' responsibilities are clearly defined by the Constitution (legislative work, monitoring the cabinet's activities, approving the central government budget). Parliamentary civil servants are obliged to support this work in the best possible manner. As the provided resources are always limited, it is necessary to concentrate and focus them on appropriate issues.

The selection of appropriate issues is necessary on a continual basis, both in long-term planning and regarding personal choices in daily work. To be able to make these choices, and to ensure efficient activities, jointly defined concrete objectives are required, for the purpose of steering daily functions and operational development. In addition to clearly defined objectives, people must be aware of the current resource status and its development needs, in order to focus development on currently appropriate targets.

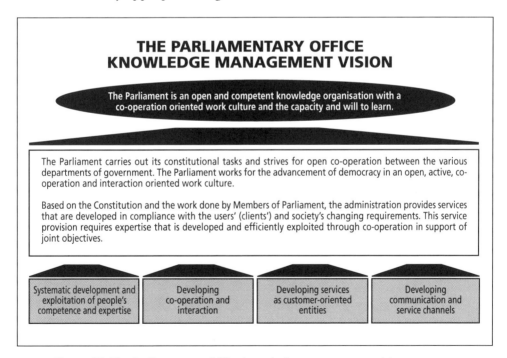

Picture 35. The Parliamentary Office knowledge management vision

The vision described in picture 35 is intended to summarise an ideal future state of affairs that is actively pursued and supported through vigorous development measures.

The IS&KM Project's Steering Group defined the following operational objectives for parliamentary knowledge management:

- To enhance and support the Parliament's and MPs' possibilities for action.

- To facilitate and accelerate the identification of required essential information and knowledge, thus enhancing the decision-making process

- To promote flexibility of activities and the erosion of organisational boundaries by supporting personal competence and expertise development plus the distribution and dissemination of tacit knowledge.

Competence and expertise are the Parliament's key resources that enable it to ensure the availability of essential, correct knowledge and its applicability, when and where required.

Correspondingly, the teams' and interviewers' observations highlighted knowledge dissemination and knowledge exploitation as the central areas in knowledge management.

As one essential part of the IS&KM Project we defined the KM target stage towards which different actors in the Parliament have to strive for. It is based on observations obtained from the teamwork and interviews conducted. Picture 36 is a description of this KM target stage pertaining to the various dimensions of a knowledge organisation.

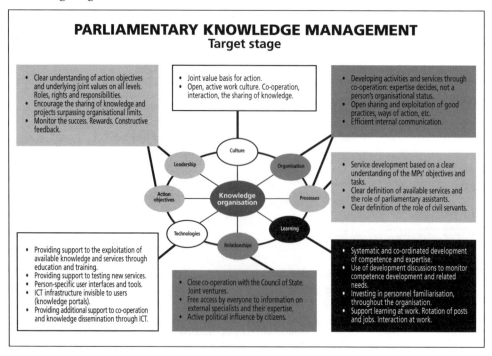

Picture 36. Target stage of parliamentary knowledge management

Operational objectives and leadership during target stage

During the IS&KM Project, the interviews and teamwork clearly indicated a number of development needs related to leadership skills. People do have the ability to manage issues but people management is far more challenging. Participants expressed the wishes to receive systematic training in this regard.

Operational objectives, and values alike, must be clearly defined and understood on all levels of action, in order to ensure a uniform, reliable standard of action, and correct course of development. The Parliament's civil service personnel must define joint shared values to support co-operation and knowledge sharing activities. While striving towards the target stage, it is advisable to base efforts on the value discussion that was launched recently in conjunction with management training, and to extend it to the various levels of the organisation. This would be the way to genuinely commit people to joint shared values on a wide basis.

In parliamentary activities, reliability is invariably the central value to be observed in leadership and all action. This value occasionally conflicts with efficiency requirements. Leadership may support the management and sharing of knowledge by clearly expressing the knowledge management objectives and benefits in a form for people to understand in their daily duties. Naturally, a careful analysis must precede expression, to eliminate mutually contradictory elements. Operational objectives are used to encourage people to enhance co-operation and knowledge sharing activities. Implementation of the said objectives must also be monitored and positive action rewarded in various ways. Constructive feedback is to be used to promote the desired type of work culture.

The work of the Parliamentary Office's Office Commission depends largely on knowledge sharing and co-operation. This refers to projects that surpass organisational boundaries and are launched in co-operation, with clearly defined responsibilities for co-ordination and development. The focus of the work of the management team is more and more shifting towards action planning and systematic monitoring. The meetings are geared towards discussing the issues under progress in various departments, and the potential for co-operation.

The aim is to identify benefits to be gained through knowledge sharing on all organisation levels, including the individuals. This will lead to increased motivation to promote co-operation.

With regard to operational development, all co-operation objectives are actively considered and people encouraged to commit themselves to joint activities.

In leadership and management activities, values are of major importance. The current parliamentary civil service organisation has strong values that are based on its long-term tradition and service concept defined as follows: "Do it immediately and well." Nevertheless, value discussion has continually been under progress, for example, during a management-training seminar in January 2001. The plan for internal communication (Publications by the Parliamentary Office 4/2000) suggests the following as joint values for the Parliament:
- Openness
- Reliability
- Predictability
- Flexibility
- Willingness to serve
- Co-operation.

The above values are to provide a basis for further action. Their importance will be consolidated through the development efforts that have been embarked upon. A target-stage work culture is typically open and active, one that supports co-operation, interaction, and the sharing of knowledge. Work culture development is supported by shared values. Once the shared values have been internalised throughout the organisation, all its activities will be steered by these values.

6.5 MPs' Knowledge Management vision 2004
MP's personal mission

People's ability to cope with the increasing deluge of information is probably the most difficult knowledge management problem. Regarding this problem, a team of MPs decided to propose a new approach where each MP individually defines his or her own personal mission. Subsequently, these definitions would be used as aids in various KM processes. A mission is an MP's personal description of the essentials and core interest areas in his or her work. In particular, MPs would apply their missions to organising their work, and to external communication. The picture is a summary of MP Markku Markkula's personal mission and core interest areas.

Picture 37: MP Markku Markkula's personal mission and core interest areas

The mission provides the parliamentary organisation with knowledge that can be used as the basis of targeting its knowledge and information provision, as well as prioritising required support. The mission will also help the organisation provide individual services next to the mass production cost level.

Among others, the MP's mission can be exploited in the following areas:

- to organise MPs' personal work,
- database structures,
- e-mail organisation,
- paper document archives,
- to facilitate co-operation between MPs and their personal assistants,
- to acquaint personal assistants with the MPs' duties, to indicate the focal points,
- to provide a joint knowledge and information storage method,
- to facilitate co-operation between MPs and civil servants,
- to describe an MP's duties, to indicate the core areas,
- to enable proactive measures; for example, the information system management can produce ready-made database structures and organise tailor-made monitoring for desired information sources,
- to support in-house expert development, such as library services.

Each MP will be personally responsible for producing his or her mission image. The objective is to produce the missions in accordance with a joint standard template, thus improving the missions' applicability, for example in the servants' work. Mission production is voluntary. A good idea would be to produce two mission versions—a detailed version for personal use and a more general one for the civil servants. It is to be expected that the models will be distributed according to the good practice principle, with production gaining momentum as people realise how many personal, high-standard services they can obtain through it.

The concept of mission is used in the majority of existing reform programmes to define the premises and to steer resource provision.

KM vision 2004

As a backbone for future development efforts, the MP team sketched a vision of the KM activities' target stage in 2004. In the spring of 2003, a new electoral period will begin in our Parliament. This provides a natural occasion to implement major changes in parliamentary information systems and related software. 2004 has been chosen as the vision time span, due to the fact that the elected MPs will then have worked for 12 months and will have, to a certain degree, established personal routines. A practical principle is that each MP is to progress towards the target stage outlined in this vision at their own pace, and to the extent they personally see fit.

The MP team summarised the following factors and principles as the KM vision corner stones:

1. Each MP will have a clear mission.
2. Openness promotes democracy and the citizens' interest in politics.
3. An MP's own professional development is target-oriented.
4. An MP's work is innovative.
5. Civil servants will have an increasing role as MP support.
6. Knowledge acquisition and information retrieval will be fast and efficient.

The other KM vision areas are as follows: The information deluge has been brought under control, work is less location dependent, the physical environment supports knowledge sharing and privacy, ICT support is mainly communal and partly personified, MPs are active networking operators, tacit knowledge is exploited with increasing efficiency, MPs can influence legislative work at the preparatory stage. Personal assistants have a clearly defined significant role in the acquisition, processing and distribution of knowledge. Learning is an important and well-functioning part of MPs' work. Parliamentary work promotes knowledge society development.

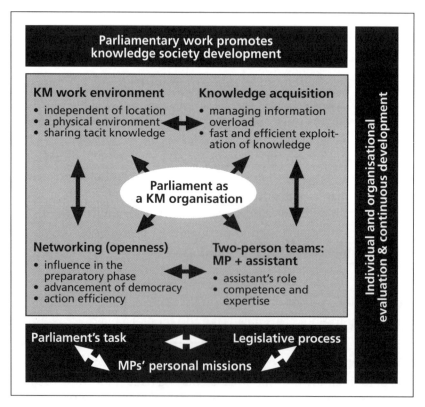

Picture 38. MP's KM vision 2004—main factors and activity areas in parliamentary KM

The above partial areas were described in detail so as to enable the various parliamentary operators to perceive the direction of required action and the benefits to be gained. Thus, the vision was adopted as the basis for implementation.

Personal Knowledge Management Toolbox

The idea of a personal knowledge management toolbox for MPs was expressed during the Committee for the Future's Technology Assessment Project. To enable the practical implementation of this idea, Markku Markkula, MP, defined the essential elements to be contained in the toolbox system. His analysis was based on the experience received interviewing the MPs to define their personal missions, plus the preparatory stage results of a number of associated pilot projects. An MP's professional development is based on the same principles as that of any other knowledge worker. This means that it is natural to initially define an overall basic frame of reference and not embark on specifying parliamentary applications until the pilot projects' results have been received.

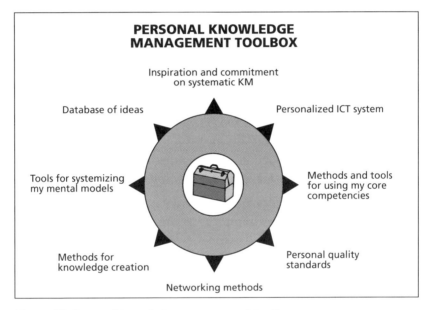

Picture 39: Personal knowledge management toolbox

The following universal principle constitutes the premise: The only way to successfully improve an individual's competence development is through his or her own commitment to the creation and long-term updating of his or her personal knowledge management toolbox. This means the adoption of a lifelong passion to learn, along with a systematic Knowledge Management (KM) lifestyle. As a result, continuous development of his or her personal talents and work methods will be integrated into the exploitation of co-operation skills in various interactive networks using the latest information and communication technologies (ICT).

There are certain significant, mutually interactive areas of professional development that have not been adequately observed. These can be highlighted through full-scale exploitation of current ICT developments. Thus, the objectives will be: 1) to identify and systematically implement those development steps that emphasise an individual's personal responsibility, and 2) to distinguish the needs for change in the work community's work culture, in addition to pursuing a systematic KM policy.

A strategic KM approach and method of action requires a determined effort. The toolbox diagram is a summary with eight central tool development target areas that are necessary to obtain adequate results. Put in a nutshell, they are as follows:

- Commitment to the systematic exploitation of ICT will provide the premise to fuel sustained activities, along with the individual's personal enthusiasm, especially his or her passion to learn and create new things. A way of life that leads to discovery learning will be crucial in the present era of networking, in terms of productivity and personal endurance alike. People can receive invigorating feedback from their fellows by implementing the results of their discoveries in practical life, thus distributing the benefits to others.

- Producing a personal ICT system for an individual calls for developing work methods that are personally suitable for him or her, plus customising the tools to his or her preference. What is essential to these activities is that everything must be carefully planned and documented. However, people must not do everything themselves; there are several co-operation processes that will ensure positive results.

- Above all, use of the personal toolbox will focus on the individual's own core competence areas. This means that the methods' and tools' development will take place in the individual's own areas of content strength, which will also facilitate the creation of new methods.

- Personal toolbox development will be based on generating one's own "quality standards" and communicating them to one's partners. Primarily, this is a question of partners becoming acquainted with one another's ICT cultures, which will allow them to benefit from other people's materials and methods.

- It is justified to say that networking has become a way of life. The best networks are based on profound co-operation, that is the joy of giving and taking—genuine joint activities and learning together. Conventional interaction, which consists of taking turns in influencing, will not be enough. Openness and trust, which are the basic KM values, are visible in all activities and provide the preconditions for innovation activities and maintaining a joint knowledge and expertise space on a continual basis. This will considerably expand the available knowledge and expertise space.

- The capacity for innovation is probably the ultimate success factor for organisations and nations alike. Software developments are continually providing new opportunities to model various matters and phenomena. Compared to working alone and in conventional teams, there is now an opportunity for genuine joint activities. This is based on utilising a joint, network-based platform and common, illustrative process descriptions, which can inspire increasing numbers of people to join mutual brainstorming for collective benefit.

- Individuals can use their personal toolboxes most effectively to create and illustratively document their personal models of thought and action by exploiting various graphics programs and visual software packages. The core of the toolbox is constituted by mental action models that are easy to edit for various situations and themes, thus enabling continuous, systematic development of one's own models of thought and action.

- Simultaneous processing of several projects is a characteristic feature in innovation. Some consist of stressful, productive stages of work; some take place in idea incubators; some are being processed jointly by several people within networks; some are waiting for a vital component to mature, while others are being finalised, etc. One of the most exacting areas of the toolbox consists of having the endurance to document ideas and maintain one's own "bank of ideas", as well as one that is shared by others, at least partially.

All of these toolbox components require personal investment that is, above all, focused on content development, software development, and on exploiting the new opportunities provided by other ICT developments. Significant differences often emerge between people due to available support services, accessibility of developer networks, and the co-operation methods applied.

When developing a model toolbox for MPs, it is advisable to produce a number of practical examples. For this purpose, we have requested that a few MPs process their personal toolboxes. This will enable us to optimise the level of the required support services, hardware, and software. As we see it, the crucial question is: How much time and effort is an individual MP prepared to spend on developing his or her personal toolbox on a long-term basis? The experience to be gained can be made available in due time to all MPs for further distribution and dissemination, including any foreseeable benefits or problems.

6.6 Development areas and projects

During the IS&KM Project, work processes were examined in the light of their overall objectives. The following questions were the ones guiding the project: What are the key issues in maintaining and developing activities to reach the joint objectives?

Which knowledge management means and measures are significant when striving for the objectives?

Development activities during the coming years will be based on the defined KM target stage and the KM vision 2004. The selected areas must be used as focal points for development with active measures being taken in the areas in question. In addition, a separate management-training programme must be launched to actively promote people's managerial skills and methods and their leadership culture.

For parliamentary knowledge management to be successful, it is extremely important to define the development areas and implement those projects that promote the desired change. The development areas are as follows:

1. Develop competence and expertise

The central resources, which support parliamentary work, are competence, expertise and their effective exploitation. Since the average age of the parliamentary civil service personnel is comparatively high, the continuation of high-quality activities is threatened by the personnel's retirement. To be able to guarantee sustained activities, it is important to ensure the individuals' competence and expertise, its systematic development, and its transfer to the possession of the organisation on a broad basis.

As the MPs and their assistants clearly stated during the team interviews, this is also, to a large extent, a question of each individual's willingness and commitment to long-term development of his or her personal work methods and habits. The pilot projects to be launched will also be geared towards developing a so-called tool kit action model.

2. Develop co-operation and interaction

The objective is to generate a co-operation and interaction culture that supports practical needs (and goals) for action.

3. Develop services into client-oriented entities

The objective is to describe the services provided by the Parliamentary Office as an entity, thus enabling the development of service provision with minimum exploitation of available resources, focusing on appropriate issues. The premises for service descriptions and goal-oriented development are the clients' needs and the service objectives formulated by the management. The MPs' mission and vision descriptions provide the basis for further specification of the service needs. These can be used, for example, to specify information service needs on a person-by-person basis.

4. Develop communication and service channels

The objective is co-ordinated development of the various communication and service channels: technological and functional services, making them user-friendly, easy to identify and easy to access. When developing the service channels, the wide variety of user needs and competence levels among the MPs and parliamentary personnel must be taken into account. The objective is to produce a user-oriented communication and service portal.

Regardless of the high availability of ICT tools in the Parliament, all users are not fully prepared to exploit the full variety of their benefits. Systematic utilisation of these tools is also impaired by high organisational boundaries and the lack of joint objectives. Joint objectives and the erosion of organisation boundaries would encourage people to share their knowledge and experience with others.

The following diagram shows how the various focal points for development (development areas) cover the knowledge creation phases.

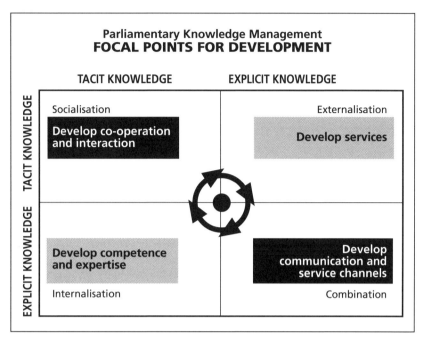

Picture 40. Focal points for development

The table below shows the development areas and related projects.

Development areas and associated projects
1. Develop competence and expertise
1.1   Describe the knowledge management and training process
1.2   Develop training provision
1.3   Transfer the individuals' competence and expertise into the organisation's possession
1.4   Training provision and learning environments
1.5   Internet-based information services: Familiarisation, training, and content-oriented support for knowledge retrieval
2. Develop co-operation and interaction
2.1 Describe the co-operation and interaction needs
• Parliamentary Office
2.2 Technological solutions to promote co-operation and interaction
• Survey
• Pilot projects
3. Develop services
3.1 Consolidate the service needs based on MPs' need definitions (visions & missions)
3.2 Describe services—overall description of MPs' service provision
4. Develop communication and service channels
4.1 Develop the Intranet's content structure and services
4.2 Define development of Intranet-based information services
4.3 Knowledge monitoring and screening services
4.4 Digital transmission of TV programmes
4.5 Mobile communication

In addition to the above projects, the MP team proposed the launching of the following pilot projects with special emphasis on the MPs' perspective:

- Mobile terminal devices as MPs' personal tools
- E-databases for MPs
- User surveys and software experiments
- Web-based working methods

The pilot projects, in which about 30 MPs are involved, were launched in January 2002. A special objective of these pilot projects is co-ordinated development of the various service channels in the Parliament: technological and functional services, making them user-friendly, easy to identify and easy to access. When developing the service channels, the wide variety of user needs and competence levels among MPs and parliamentary personnel must be taken into account.

 Practical knowledge management consists of exploiting the individuals' personal strengths, competence and expertise for the organisation's benefit. It involves the enabling of joint learning, exploitation of good practices, continuous follow-up, seizing and provision of knowledge, encouragement, plus the creation and sharing of knowledge, competence and expertise.

7. Summary

One of the tasks assigned to the Committee for the Future is to get acquainted with the methods of future studies and to assess the societal impact of technology. One of the technology assessment projects organised during the years 2000-2001 by the Committee has been "Knowledge Management" with special emphasis on changes effecting work culture and working methods. In addition to this, the Committee has exploited new information and communication technological methods in several ways in its own activities.

In a broader sense the Parliament has taken special activities in developing its own knowledge management. The IS&KM Project (Information Systems and Knowledge Management) carried out in 2000-2001 was geared towards defining a joint content and reference framework for knowledge management, to create a vision of knowledge management in the Parliament, and to consolidate the various operative objectives for knowledge management. The project assessed the available means to reach the objectives, and defined solution proposals for a concrete revision programme. Several pilot projects have been started to implement these proposals. Among others, the Committee for the Future operates as a test unit for the new emerging knowledge management methods.

The purpose of this book is to present our views of knowledge management, and to describe the various processes that we have used in our Parliament to outline and analyse the role and importance of knowledge management, its essential components and application in practice during the years 2000–2001.

In this publication, the expression "we" is actually not used in reference to the authors' opinions but, rather, to refer to the views of the MPs and the Parliament's civil servants who participated in these projects. The joint meetings and processes generated a shared reality of a kind, indicating the current state of affairs, and how we wish it should change towards the knowledge management vision described in this publication.

In Finland, at least, a general societal view is that national parliaments should generate preconditions for efficient, innovative activities by citizens and communities, and show examples of such activities in their own work, with the overall purpose being to improve the quality of life.

The initial spur for this book came from the Committee for the Future, from its obligation to assess the societal impacts of technology and the objective to improve its own work efficiency. For the book to serve as a Finnish contribution in international co-operation to develop the basics of democracy, parliamentarianism and parliamentary work, it is also necessary to extensively describe the Finnish Parliament's own knowledge management processes and development steps taken in this field.

Transitions from an industrial society through an information society to a society of knowledge, understanding and wisdom are major challenges for both individuals and communities. Desired results can only be achieved through determined hard work. It is society's responsibility to create equal preconditions and an inspiring atmosphere for the required change to take place. Each and every one must build a strong personal educational base for lifelong learning, one that will allow them to regenerate in view of the coming societal, occupational and personal changes in life.

In accordance with the Finnish Government's Futures Report from 1998, the citizens' competence, their skills and expertise are the only basis for Finland's success. In particular, the Government defined the following three policies:

1. Steadily increase the resources available for research and development from the year 2000 on. At the same time, seek to increase the returns from such investment.

2. Lead the transition to an information society, seeking a role in the European Union as an "information society laboratory". Use the information society as a tool for increasing Finland's human and social capital.

3. Introduce a system of lifelong learning encouraging skill enhancement and mobility during the entire individual life cycle. In business policy, emphasize quality, education, management skills and personal development.

It is extremely important that these policies were also approved by Parliament, as consolidated in the Committee for the Future's memorandum. In addition to these three national strategies, our national innovation system deserves to be highlighted as the fourth. Since the 1980s, Finland has taken determined efforts, through collaboration between the public and private sectors, to develop a national innovation system. This system is an intellectually and materially solid, versatile action environment that encourages the creation of new intuitive knowledge.

Human capital has extremely close connections with social capital, due to the fact that learning is a highly communal event and process, in addition to its strongly individual aspects. Social capital is generated by an intellectual culture, for which the action environment creates the prerequisites for birth and development. Essential components of social capital include networks, work processes, atmospheres, shared values and work methods, trust, and the capacity to think and act with other people.

Picture 41: An overview of the factors constituting Finland's determined future policies during the late 1990s and early 21st century.

This publication is based on the Committee for the Future's decisions from recent years. The Committee has adopted the habit of processing the most significant results of all TA projects. Continuity is considered extremely important. Each TA process generates a number of insights and discoveries that deserve to be processed into political action, such as conveying the challenges encountered to the consideration of other parties. Consequently, the Committee has achieved significant results through its own networked activities—we take responsibility and participate. The annex of this publication is a description of this action method of ours. It includes a summary and proposals for actions that were accepted by the Committee.

The experiences of MPs, as well as conclusions from some outside evaluations, have convinced us that technology as-

> Motto: We must work together and create joint continuous change processes for the future.

sessment projects must primarily be interpreted as joint learning processes for MPs and various experts. Furthermore, each assessment project naturally produces a report document for use by all MPs and other interested parties. Assessment processes produce tacit knowledge that can be used to get acquainted with technological solutions and related values choices. How the values are selected will decisively affect the possibilities of contributing to the work culture through knowledge. We are constantly involved in the future building process. The TA Steering Group emphasises that we must work jointly for the future. The experts and decision-makers must jointly create a language that can be used to generate effective wisdom. Wisdom does not work through statements alone. It will emerge from working together. This means that assessment activities are future-creative efforts, not mere collections of facts and expert statements for use by MPs.

Chapter 2 outlines the multifaceted theme to include phenomena using which the effects of technology can be managed and exploited. This meant that values, learning and goal-oriented activities materialised as the core knowledge management issues. These are elements of lifelong learning. A citizen of the future must learn to know, learn to do, learn to live together, learn to be, and learn to choose. These learning dimensions must be consolidated on a practical level to enable people to cope with the information deluge and contribute to building a culture where knowledge can be wisely managed and conducted.

Knowledge creates new knowledge. Knowledge work will involve increasing innovativeness requirements. The number of jobs based on mechanical repetition will decrease and will increasingly be replaced by work that is mentally more demanding. The profile of a knowledge professional consists of knowledge, expertise and wisdom. With an increasing amount of knowledge-intensive work in a working community, an individual will have an increasing responsibility regarding his or her own competence. Organisations will have to analyse what knowledge means to the community, what type of added value it produces, where the community's knowledge capital resides, and how to measure, evaluate and develop intangible capital assets.

Everybody is making strategies and launching projects all over Finland." This will not be enough, however. Everyone must be involved and, in addition to programmes, action and practical work processes are required to achieve desired goals. Practical work and new innovations are the activities and results, which matter the most. We, and this applies to every Finn, even have to dirty our hands, and we must get past dilly-dallying to future work and practical processes.

TA Steering Group

New technology has a major impact on the volume of knowledge, and on its processing methods. According to experts, the increasing extent of change and the possibilities for action provided to people, plus global activities, will impose increasing requirements on technological development and its exploitation. This will increase the pressure for learning and developing co-operation cultures.

Innovativeness generates innovativeness - but only in a trustworthy and trusting growth environment. To be reliable, one must rely on others. It is only in a trusting working community, which equally appreciates various knowledge contributions by different employees, that the entire available competence capacity can be successfully exploited and increased.

Asking and questioning—the attitude of positive curiosity - are also important in a future work culture. New methods must be developed for leadership, practical lifelong learning, networking, and co-operation between the public and private sectors. People can no longer be led using the methods of an industrialised society. Politicians must also modernise their work methods and become aware of the underlying values in their activities, as well as the enormous possibilities that KM offers. In the capacity of a knowledge user and knowledge creator, the individual will always be at the focal point of knowledge management.

Chapter 3 deals with the nature of knowledge and the dimensions of knowledge management. We analysed and illuminated the concepts and intend to create a joint understanding of what knowledge management means in parliamentary work. Creating a joint language is extremely important to enable innovative thinking in joint activities. Analysing and translating the concepts into plain language is very important in parliamentary co-operation and in other working life sectors. If discussions remain mere exchange of opinions, people will fail to produce such a synergy that provides ample space for joint new ideas. Therefore, the knowledge conversion and creation process introduced by professor Ikujiro Nonaka and the concept Ba (physical, mental and virtual place and space) where new knowledge is created, are dealt with to a relatively large extent. Nonaka's thinking can also be applied to the development of networking. Pondering the concept of tacit knowledge raised several proposals for the development of parliamentary work (Chapter 5). MPs are knowledge experts whose personal regeneration process is extremely important to every nation.

Chapter 4 contains a draft profile of a knowledge professional that predicts changes in job descriptions and challenges for learning. The issue is not only restricted to learning specific professional matters and information and communication technologies, but also involves the creation of a new type of work culture where innovative and goal-oriented activities are emphasised. Voluntary, ethical and innovative action in extensive international networks calls for a redefinition of the relationship between employers and employees. Dialogue, i.e. a learning discussion between different people is important, both face-to-face and through virtual arrangements.

Educating people in creativity and responsibility from early childhood is a serious challenge to an information society. To achieve this goal, we must aim for a knowledge society. If we don't pay enough attention to learning processes and to the challenging work culture, the workload will be too heavy and our visions will not come true. The effects of technology may take future generations in a direction where the said extensive interaction and networking will decrease rather than increase. The knowledge professionals of a future information society will have to master three major themes and develop these throughout their lives. Knowledge is something that we already have, what will be required are the capabilities to apply and exploit knowledge, to get along with people from different cultural backgrounds, and to learn responsible finance management on both personal and societal levels.

Work is changing into the provision of services, which means that mechanical work will not be enough. At the same time, business will be conducted globally and virtually, and in an increasingly individual-oriented fashion, in accordance with the customer's wishes and requirement. This means that all employees must think for themselves. Knowledge is created by doing and by joint processes, it does not exist somewhere ready-made for mechanical distribution to others.

Three major lifelong themes for people—starting from school age:

1. Networking capabilities—soft and hard

2. Business capabilities—soft and hard

3. Competence development capabilities—soft and hard

These are the subjects and capabilities that we shall need in future. All the rest we can obtain from the ICT virtual reality that surrounds us. Future competence requires abilities to grow into an expert. This growth begins at home from early childhood. Humanity is a lifelong learning process—the same applies to openness and democracy. If we don't learn that giving means getting and not losing, we can only achieve a fraction of what our brain and sense capacity allows us to have. We need to use jointly the full capacity of our complex human minds. By understanding and applying this, we begin the journey to ourselves and to the appreciation and management of our humanity.

TA Steering Group

In parliamentary work just-on-time knowledge is required. Mere general statistical information will not be enough to serve future citizens who will be in a better position to easily approach the decision-makers through the Internet and mobile phones. Knowledge must be created in problem-solving situations here and now. Therefore, each and everyone must be capable of acquiring, processing and distributing it by themselves. Knowledge is also, and particularly, created through joint activities and learning. This will necessitate learning new methods in parliamentary work, and in public administration in general.

Co-operation is a future challenge. Naturally, this has always been true; however, it will contain a number of additional paradoxes: co-operation must be increasingly individual but more extensive, increasingly faster but more innovative, increasingly productive but more ethical.

In terms of regional politics, various centres of excellence i.e. innovative environments, will be significant factors in a knowledge society for wealth creation both locally and nationally. Learning regions of this type will have the best prerequisites for success in a changing world. In an innovative environment, working relationships are often networks and networks "emerge" from the environment. Centres of excellence of this type must be exploited for the benefit of the entire nation, which will call for the wise management of knowledge, expertise and skills. One of the challenges to regional development in a knowledge society is to guarantee a sufficient quality of life and technological infrastructure to the people who spend part of their lives outside the said innovative centres of growth.

The factors that affect the birth of a networked economy manifest themselves as cultural, social and structural changes. In general, a network is thought of as an interconnected entity of mutually independent components. A successful network will be based on intellectual entrepreneurship, co-operation skills, and efficient distribution and exploitation of knowledge and competence developed by various actors. People's personal activity will be emphasised. Inside the production and consumer sectors, and between them as well, an interactive networked economy will emerge with multifaceted effects.

Knowledge networks change work cultures

Learning is co-operation since nobody can alone exploit all the opportunities encountered. Effective sharing of information and knowledge networks have essentially changed the work culture from working alone into joint activities and learning together, i.e. building a shared knowledge reality, which is actively used by all those involved.

This joint culture can be born only through determined efforts and open interaction. Technology may enable an efficient network but an intellectual network can develop only through co-operation and inspiring other people.

TA Steering Group

In a global economy with decreasing geographic obstacles for locating business activities, and fewer restrictions on the free movement of people between countries, a well-functioning society is an essential success factor in competition. The success of the Finnish economy and society will decisively depend on public sector's management capabilities, in other words, how successful we are on building public-private partnerships and encouraging atmosphere for deep-going co-operation, in general. Keeping the public sector finance healthy is a special challenge that requires, above all, investing in the future, which must be done, however, in compliance with the citizens' wishes and expectations, both in short-term service development and with respect to sustainable development.

Chapter 5 summarises the viewpoints of knowledge management, and the means to the regeneration and creation of new knowledge through using a Knowledge Management Dynamo. This dynamo will provide a continuous regeneration process through values and learning exploiting the knowledge society's methodical opportunities and joint activities. With the KM Dynamo components up and running, a continual movement will be generated to sustain the regeneration process. Starting up the various components requires professional and ethical solutions, both from individuals and from the community involved. The KM Dynamo will provide MPs with an excellent tool to create a personal mission in co-operation with citizens and experts. The work method can be, for example, using an MP's personal competence for legislative work in co-operation with government officials.

The end of Chapter 5 describes in brief a number of various working methods and ideas for the development of parliamentary knowledge management activities. The proposals concern information and communication technologies and their use, development of co-operation, and building a knowledge management toolbox for MPs.

The parliament now makes extensive use of ICT. Chapter 6 describes the highlights of the processes carried out in order to implement the latest developments of knowledge management within the Parliament. Over the years, parliamentary basic functions and data processing have become integrated to such a degree that it is now difficult, or virtually impossible, to tell them apart. On the one hand, this will provide new opportunities for knowledge management. On the other hand, indulging in extremely sophisticated state-of-the-art ICT solutions may obstruct the sound development of these activities.

Parliamentary activities are characterised by a high task performance rate, their partly unpredictable, comprehensive and multidimensional nature, and the mobility of MPs. A significant feature in KM activities is the personal work culture of each MP, his or her individual ICT work method, as well as co-operation and division of labour between MPs and their assistants. All of these factors impose a special requirement on the processing and management of knowledge.

The premise for an in-depth analysis of the KM principles, and their implementation in Parliament, was the awareness that we can develop our work processes to a significant degree. To enable the MPs to promote the desired development towards a knowledge society, it is absolutely necessary that they personally act at the forefront of development, in certain respects, at least. Thus, they would also personally understand, through their own experiences, the opportunities provided by ICT, as well as the difficulties encountered in practical application.

Networking, multicultural aspects, and the erosion of boundaries are making legislative work increasingly demanding. Legislators must keep abreast of development, more strictly than ever. Technology has a major role to play with respect to answering the challenges of ever more complex work processes. Knowledge professionals require advanced hardware and software in order to have the possibility to work anywhere, at a time that suits them best in each situation.

The knowledge management vision of the Parliamentary Office was defined as follows: "The Parliament is an open and competent knowledge organisation with a co-operation oriented work culture and capacity and will to learn." Naturally, this vision was converted into specific development objectives pertaining to each partial KM area, including the action to be taken. To enable progress in the selected direction, it was decided to launch a number of pilot projects, and to define the most appropriate routes, both operationally and economically, based on the experience of the pilots. Determined efforts will be made during the next few years to change activities as specified. The objective of the pilot projects is co-ordinated development of the various communication and service channels: technological and functional services, making them user-friendly, easy to identify and easy to access. When developing the service channels, the wide variety of user needs and competence levels among the MPs and parliamentary personnel must be taken into account. One of the objectives is to develop further and also personalise workstations and user-oriented communication and service portals.

About 30 MPs from a total of 200 will participate in the pilot projects, plus a number of civil servants. The key principle is every participant's personal will to get acquainted with the new opportunities, and to spend a considerable amount of time on this effort. Towards the end of 2002, the results will be used to make the final decisions regarding which hardware and software items to install following the 2003 Parliamentary Election, which KM support functions to replace and which KM processes to develop. To maintain democratic functionality, it is crucial that optimal working conditions be created for our MPs and civil servants, even when compared to all other knowledge professionals.

In this publication, we have concentrated on describing a number of processes that can be used to achieve new knowledge and competence. These are processes that can be promoted, without hesitation, for use by individuals, organisations and society alike. Knowledge management provides a variety of opportunities; however, it also requires the definition of joint objectives, plus determined efforts to achieve these objectives.

The TA Steering Group produced a definition of knowledge management that also serves as a conclusion of the required attitude, skills and actions that will be needed in the future:

- Knowledge management means discovery learning.
- Knowledge management is an issue, which involves the wise care and development of knowledge, skills and communication based on a desired vision of the future.
- Knowledge management is based on shared values defined through a joint process.
- Knowledge management requires innovative, responsible leadership.

This definition was born from the need to find a joint language, place and space for learning—Ba—where the Steering Group was able to outline and develop parliamentary knowledge work beyond political party boundaries and views. The purpose of this definition is not to gain control over the issue, but to enable dissemination of jointly learned, outlined and wisely managed knowledge. A working method of this type requires openness and trust.

As we see it, Parliament is currently engaged in a determined development of its own activities, in accordance with these decisions. At the same time, as the decision by the Committee for the Future included in the annex, clearly indicates, MPs must promote the desired course of development in society in several ways. In particular, they must proactively influence the prevailing attitudes and work culture development.

What man wants is to be successful, to achieve quality in his work and gain success in life in general. People are currently aware of the opportunities available for this, and increasingly prepared to make determined efforts to reach their objectives. There will be increasing openness to clearly display these goals. People will be increasingly aware that they must request help from others, and help others at the same time. Success will be achieved together through networking.

In knowledge work, new applications of ICT have made possible a total paradigm shift from individual-based work to effective working together up to the level of building and using a shared knowledge reality, which is based on joint mental models, and which is constantly further developed through effective team work and team learning. Continuous upgrading of personal mastery is more and more targeted to competence development within work processes. Personal mastery is also dedicated to assisting the other members of networked teams to achieve desired goals—we can accomplish more by working together. These are the functional features that we shall be practising in Parliament in conjunction with the pilot projects launched early in 2002. The projects are focused on increasing ICT mobility, adopting web-based working methods and personalising workstations and the working habits of MPs.

This paradigm shift, and the related changes in work cultures and work methods, will be increasingly highlighted during the next few years, even on the parliamentary level, especially if and when we as MPs want to make our nation one of the most competitive in the world. And, what we want to stress here is that competitiveness means, above all, long-term commitment to increase the quality of life of all our citizens.

Markku Markkula, MP

References

CHAPTER II

1 Handy 1995.
2 Koski 1999.
3 Holma & Lappalainen & Pilkevaara 1997; Wiig, 1997; Liebowitz & Beckman 1998; KM-ohjausryhmä 2000.
4 VN 1997.
5 Tuomi 1999.
6 Tuomi 1999.
7 Teikari 1999.
8 Otala 1999.
9 Otala 1999; Ståhle 2000; Nonaka 2000.
10 Pehrman 2000.
11 Koski 1999; Koivula, & Teikari 1996; Savolainen & Himanen 1995.
12 Kuusi 1989; Luukkainen 2000.
13 Levomäki 1999.

CHAPTER III

14 Holma & Lappalainen & Pilkevaara 1997; Aho & Leppänen & Tamminen 1998.
15 Holma & Lappalainen & Pilkevaara 1997; Wiig, 1997; Liebowitz & Beckman 1998; KM-ohjausryhmä 2000.
16 Kaivo-Oja & Kuusi 1999.
17 Hautamäki 1996; Kuusi 1986.
18 Kuusi 1986.
19 Holma & Lappalainen & Pilkevaara1997; Liebowitz & Beckman 1998.
20 Holma & Lappalainen & Pilkevaara1997.
21 Nonaka 1991; Holma & Lappalainen & Pilkevaara 1997.
22 Holma & Lappalainen & Pilkevaara 1997; Niiniluoto 1989; Kasvi & Vartiainen 2000; Allee 1997.
23 Niiniluoto 1989; Kasvi & Vartiainen 2000.
24 Niiniluoto 1989.
25 Kuusi 1986.
26 Wikström et al. 1994.
27 Niiniluoto 1989.
28 Niiniluoto 1989.
29 Nonaka & Toyama & Konno 2000.
30 Kasvi & Vartiainen 2000.
31 Kasvi & Vartiainen 2000.
32 Ministry of Labour 1999.
33 Polanyi 1958.
34 Nonaka 1991.
35 Sveiby 1997.
36 Raivola & Vuorensyrjä 1998.
37 Nonaka & Toyama & Konno 2000; Jaspers 1953.
38 Nonaka & Toyama & Konno 2000.
39 Nonaka & Takeuchi 1995; Kulkki 1996; Kalthoff & Nonaka & Nueno 1997; Nonaka & Konno 1998; Nonaka & Umemoto & Sasaki 1998; Nonaka & Toyama & Konno 2000; von Krogh & Nonaka & Nishiguchi 2000.
40 Nonaka 1991.
41 Nonaka 1991; Suurla 1998.
42 Nonaka 2000.
43 Nonaka & Toyama & Konno 2000.
44 Nonaka & Toyama & Konno 2000.
45 VATT 2000.

CHAPTER IV

46 Csikszentmihalyi 1996; Davenport ja Prusak 1998; Kilpi 2000; Koski 1999; Kyrö 1998; Nonaka 2000; Raivola & Vuorensyrjä 1998; Stewart 1997.
47 Kilpi 2000; Cortada 1998.
48 Kilpi 2000.
49 Kilpi 2000.
50 Davenport & Prusak 1998.
51 Kyrö 1998, 2000.
52 Csikszentmihalyi 1996; Koski 1999; Markkula & Suurla 1997; Nonaka 2000.
53 Csikszentmihalyi 1996; Kilpi 2000; Koski 1999.
54 Koski 1999.
55 Järvinen 2000.
56 Järvinen 2000.
57 Järvinen 2000.
58 Raivola & Vuorensyrjä 1998; Stewart 1997.
59 Raivola & Vuorensyrjä 1998; Negroponte 2000.
60 Kilpi 2000.
61 Kilpi 1999 ja 2000.
62 Ogbeide 2000.
63 Ogbeide 2000; Markkula & Suurla 1998.
64 Suurla et al. 1999.
65 Rogers 1983; Lampikoski 1997; Botkin et al. 1981; Suurla & Markkula & Finnish Leonardo Centre. 1999.
66 Ogbeide 2000.
67 Autio-Tuuli & al. 2000.
68 Ståhle & Grönroos 1998.
69 Ministry of Labour 1999.
70 Ministry of Labour 1999.
71 Castells 1996; Väyrynen 1999; Kostiainen 2000.
72 Kostiainen 2000.
73 Kostiainen 2000.
74 Kilpi 2000; Autio 2000.
75 Cohen & Levinthal 1990; Nahapiet & Ghoshal 1998.
76 Autio 2000.
77 Autio 2000.
78 Ministry of Labour 1999.
79 Karivalo 2000.
80 Halme 2000.

CHAPTER V

81 Suurla & Markkula & Finnish Leonardo Centre 1999.
82 Frösén 2000; Mustajärvi 2000; Vilavaara 2000; Tiihonen 2000.
83 Suurla & Markkula & Finnish Leonardo Centre 1999.
84 Kaivo-Oja & Kuusi 2000.
85 Raivola & Vuorensyrjä 1998.
86 Nonaka & Toyama & Konno 2000.

Annex:
Decision by the Committee for the Future: Conclusions and proposals for action based on the TA Project

The experts that contributed to this Technology Assessment Project were unanimous on the importance of openness and learning together. However, the issue will remain mere talk unless we are able to develop concrete methods through which all parties can win. Joint activities, the growth of mutual reliance capital and improving joint learning can never be achieved unless each and everyone start with themselves. This meant that the TA Project's Steering Group members, who were assigned by the Parliament's Committee for the Future, also started the required knowledge management development activities with themselves. The project was launched through joint working seminars where a development programme was jointly outlined.

Implementation of this programme has already started. The objective is, in addition to producing more accurate personal activity profiles, to develop the Parliament's knowledge management by exploiting creativity, dialogues, participating learning, etc. (see Chapters 5 and 6).

Work cultures must be changed in Finland / Insights by the TA Steering Group:

- Long-term success can only be achieved through developing the communal aspects of work. Deliberate measures must be taken to develop the working communities' internal culture and working methods towards joint learning, and to increase networking in their activities. Partners must be sought beyond conventional boundaries, from a variety of action environments and cultures.

- Successful networking requires that the individual in question becomes aware of his or her personal mission and its underlying values. These are the means to generate new solutions. What will emerge is a sustained process: people develop technology, and technology will provide new opportunities challenging the pioneers to develop themselves. Values and value-related discussion must not be detached from the working communities' and individuals' long-term vocational development and lifelong learning.

- Significant innovations will be produced, especially by combining in-depth knowledge, expertise and experience from various fields. We must launch forums for the exchange of experience where contrasting views are heard, applied and jointly illustrated for new sectors.

- Information and communication technologies, and information services, are not enough to guarantee the success of the activities pursued, no matter how efficient they are. Major financial investments will also prove insufficient, unless the users become committed proponents and developers of the required knowledge acquisition and knowledge management methods. New ideas and innovations are disseminated through internal agents of change, not by increasing and flooding information.

- As technology enables people, as citizens, municipality members and employees, and as a variety of human communities, to take a stand in matters that do or do not concern them, this challenge must be accepted. Trust depends on hearing people, and on their participation, not on commands and instructions issued from higher levels. We have reason to consider complementing the model of representational democracy that has been in use for thousands of years.

The purpose of this Technology Assessment Project has been, on one hand, to provide the Parliament with the required knowledge on knowledge management, and, on the other, to serve as a promoting process for personal learning for MPs. To enable the views generated by the project to change development in Finland as desired, the Steering Group defined the acceleration and progress of desired measures as its main objective.

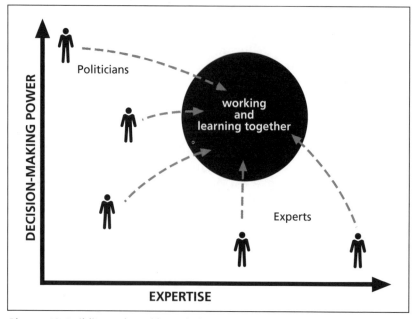

Picture 42: Building a shared knowledge reality

This report is not a conventional summary of results. Instead, co-operation partners were sought during the project, who would be prepared to promote the following measures. The ideas on the measures to be taken, and the organisations responsible for subsequent projects were expressed in the Steering Group seminars, during educational visits, and in meeting discussions.

It is far easier to organise own projects than agree with other parties on steps to be taken by them. The role of the Committee for the Future is to express its well-grounded vision of the direction of future developments, and, especially, to get the others to launch such measures as it considers necessary, and to monitor their progress for the purpose of providing parliamentary decision-making with useful knowledge and experience.

In its reports, the Committee for the Future emphasises the role of networking and active co-operation as progenitors of social innovations. The Committee wants to promote the launch of the following proposals for action, and to exploit the results in its own work.

1. The Committee for the Future as an assessor of innovation activities

"Human aspect in innovation" is one of the all-permeating success factors that has been defined by the Committee for the Future. On an international scale, Finland has achieved good results through determined development of its national innovation activities. The need to increase the individuals' and communities' innovation activities was strongly emphasised in the TA Project. In its work, it is useful for the Committee for the Future to a gain deeper insight into innovation activities, by assessing the latest research findings and the so-called good practices.

a) The challenge of developing a national innovation system

In 1999, the Finnish National Fund for Research and Development SITRA launched a research programme on innovation activities. This programme is geared towards identifying the central development challenges and opportunities of the Finnish innovation system. The most significant research subject is the functioning of modern innovation processes and innovation networks. Most significant innovations emerge from co-operation between several experts and organisations.

The programme consists of 12 sub-projects. Among other things, these concentrate on investigating the differences in innovation activities between the high and low technology sectors, networking in research and development activities, sharing expertise through networks, knowledge-intensive service businesses, design's strategic importance in business life, the role of consumers in the innovation process, the dynamics of expert networks, the challenges of regulation in working life from the point of view of change and regeneration, the nature of transition in the labour market, co-operation between polytechnic institutions and business life, the incentives offered by the Finnish regulation system to innovation activities, plus the scientific basis of innovation policies. SITRA is to publish the programme results in the autumn of 2001.

> *The Committee for the Future will get deeply acquainted with the strengths and weaknesses of our national innovation system and will assess the measures required on the national level using the innovation research programme of SITRA that will be brought to completion in the autumn of 2001.*

b) Knowledge Management and regional innovation activities

Regarding Finland's success in international competition, regional innovation activities constitute an interesting point of view and a level of action with a considerable number of unexplored possibilities. The international discussions conducted during the projects (with the USA, Japan and the EU) indicated that there is wide interest in this theme. One of the points focused upon was Finland's natural role as a laboratory that provides an experience on the creation of new models of action for Knowledge Management through determined consensus between the main sectors. The national importance of this theme is also underlined by the fact that several ministries have taken action to define the content of their regional innovation policies, among other things.

In its own activities, the Committee for the Future will exploit, among other things, the "Knowledge Management and Regional Innovation Activities" project that is organised by the Finnish Association of Graduate Engineers TEK. The project, which will be carried out during 2001–2002, combines our universities' latest research findings of international standard with those activities that promote innovative spirit and new entrepreneurship and create new jobs at the regional level.

c) The role of regions and municipalities as knowledge society development promoters.

In addition to the services created through global and national societal development, the citizens' everyday life is significantly affected by the information society culture prevailing in their home municipalities. The Board of the Association of Finnish Local and Regional Authorities has defined the role of municipalities using five view points:

1. Service development,
2. Contribution of municipalities to the development of industries and employment,
3. Possibilities of influencing through local data, information and knowledge content,
4. Importance of knowledge and expertise, and
5. Economy based on efficient, cost-effective and competitive infrastructures.

The Association emphasises that each municipality must actively launch their activities with their own preconditions as the basis, to be able to benefit from the possibilities provided by an information society. Even if a joint model does not exist for these activities, help may be provided by external individual projects and their accumulated experience.

The Finnish National Fund for Research and Development SITRA has assumed the role of an organiser and supporter of projects that generate new action models. A number of pilot projects concentrating on learning regions will be launched in various parts of Finland during 2000–2001. These will apply the experience gained and the action model used by the Learning Ylä-Karjala Project. However, a number of new, entirely unexplored possibilities will also be tested, such as small-business networking and marketing, developing new industries for rural areas, electronic home help services and teletreatment for the nursing trade, citizen participation and network democracy, activities for the unemployed, preventing the exclusion of young people, development of the tourist industry and related services, plus establishment of telework centres. Subsequently, the pilot projects' experience is to be used to build a national strategy.

The Committee for the Future proposes to the Ministry of the Interior that regional associations and other relevant parties collaborate to compile the results of regional and municipal information society projects in such a fashion that the Committee can exploit the results for the preparation of its next Future Report by the Parliament, and for its other projects.

d) Generating critical mass for scientific Knowledge Management in Finland

New solutions are required in various sectors, for societal processes and business processes alike.

The role of science will gain increasing importance as social functions and societal processes become more complex. Scientific communities and related networks operate at the focal point of an information society and provide it with a pulsating flow of vital power. The EU's scientific research steering policy emphasises the user-friendliness aspects of an information society. Furthermore, technology constitutes an essential part to social innovations. The users' role as social innovation developers is becoming crucial. Technological solutions are not only generated in narrow specialist laboratories but also as part of a developed society through co-operation between experts from various fields. Documentation, adaptation and distribution of good practices into curiosity-provoking and learning-promoting models and illustrative learning and teaching materials has become a key success factor in global competition between nations.

The Committee for the Future considers it important that the Centre for Knowledge and Innovation Research of the Helsinki School of Economics and Business Administration is co-operating intensively with the said region-

al innovation project to clarify the importance of knowledge management for information society administration and regeneration processes. It is essential to create the prerequisites to generate critical mass for research and development activities in this field, and for the development of co-operation methods in Finland.

2. Future forums clarifying the role of teachers as educators and developers of methods for enthusiastic learning and joint activities

Over the past few decades, working life has changed very rapidly from working alone into teamwork and networked activities. Desired development of work community atmospheres, work cultures and working methods calls for new values, attitudes and measures. Regarding the level of national expertise and the citizens' working skills, capabilities and attitudes, for the next few decades, teachers will have a decisive role to play. This means that teachers should revise their teaching strategies to be more versatile and more encouraging towards learning to learn, and to be more supportive to learning by doing and exploring. This type of desired development can only be achieved as result of several mutually supportive measures.

The Committee for the Future will undertake preparatory action in co-operation with provincial culture departments, all other education administration units, teachers' trade unions, and other relevant parties, to organise future laboratory seminars concentrating on knowledge management and the future of work.

3. Social capital as a driving force in working life plus developing Personnel Balance Sheet concept as part of business life and other organisational activities

As activities are becoming more and more knowledge-intensive and organisations increasingly dependent on innovations, personnel resource maintenance will require a new type of vision and new methods. A conventional profit and loss account sets out the organisation's wealth (balance sheet) and its cash flow (profit and loss account). As the changes that take place in intellectual capitalare barely visible or invisible in conventional bookkeeping, businesses, in particular, have embarked on the creation of new capital assessment systems. Personnel balance sheet, as an example, is a report describing the human capital of a company.

Each community is a learning community. With the development of a knowledge society, intellectual capital has gained a crucial role among the capital assets of any learning community. It consists of three central intertwined basic elements, which are: the individual's competencies connected with the work processes, the organisation's internal culture and structures, plus the organisation's external networks.

The Committee for the Future proposes that the Ministry of Labour assess the progress of the proposals set out in the final report from 1997–1999 by its Knowledge Society Team titled "From Information Society to Knowledge-Based Society Employment by Innovation", with regard to Finland. The Committee especially proposes measures to accelerate the development and adoption of the personnel balance sheet model in Finland.

4. eLearning as a rapidly expanding business and national success factor

Several expert bodies have assessed that eLearning is currently undergoing a similar explosion of growth development as the telecommunications cluster did 10 years ago. Many things are taking place in Finland. Within the administrative sphere of the Ministry of Education, projects have been launched on virtual schools, virtual polytechnics, and virtual universities. A project launched for the production of national culture content is in progress. The Academy of Finland is in the process of launching its "New Learning Environments" research project. Several ICT businesses are already providing part of their internal personnel training using electronic learning equipment and methods, and are developing commercial services in the field. The National Technology Agency (TEKES) has included significant eLearning projects in its technology programmes. Digital television broadcasting with culture and education channels will start in the autumn of 2001. However, these measures will not be enough to keep the Finnish methods and products at the leading edge of development in the global market. Our activities are excessively Finland-focused, the steps taken are too short, and, which makes matters worse, concentrated on the domestic market. Nevertheless, Finns have excellent possibilities to become the industry's dominant developers and operators, thanks to high-level technological know-how, especially in the mobile ICT sector, and the country's educational system, which emphasises lifelong learning and is, qualitatively and globally, at the cutting edge of development.

The Committee for the Future proposes that TEKES should consider the launching of an eLearning Technology programme. The purpose of this programme would be to co-ordinate and intensify co-operation in this sector, to improve the results' dissemination and utilisation, and to multiply the development projects that are currently in progress in the field, in such a fashion that the Finnish businesses and public administration could essentially accelerate the process of converting the sector's technology, methods and contents into saleable products and could thus acquire a significant role for the Finns in the industry's global market.

5. Knowledge Management in the Parliament's own activities

One of the tasks assigned to the Committee for the Future is to get deeply acquainted with the methods of future studies and to assess the societal impact of technology. The Committee has exploited new information and communication technological methods in several ways in its own activities. The Parliament is developing its own knowledge management using Tieto-Enator Oy as a consultant. Among other things, this projects is geared towards defining a joint content and reference frame for knowledge management, to create a vision of knowledge management in the Parliament, and to consolidate the various operative objectives for knowledge management. The project will assess the available means to reach the objectives, and will define solution proposals for a concrete revision programme.

> *The Committee for the Future proposes that the principles and suggestions set out in the technology assessment report be processed by the various teams of the Parliament's Knowledge Management Project, and that the conclusions be included in the proposals for action. The Committee also proposes that itself be nominated as a test unit for the new emerging knowledge management methods.*

6. Knowledge Management EPTA's annual theme for 2001 with Finland chairing the network

The societal impact of technology is attracting increasing attention, even in parliamentary activities in the various European countries. Finland will have the chair of the EPTA network (European Parliamentary Technology Assessment <www.eptanetwork.org>) for 2001. Finland has proposed Knowledge Management as the annual theme. Among other things, the following themes will be dealt with, especially in the light of a mobile future: Network Democracy, Interoperability, Ethics and Values, eBusiness, eLearning and eAdmistration. Among the annual period's operative main issues is intensifying co-operation, especially network-based utilisation of the assessment projects carried out in various countries, plus the potential launch of joint projects. The main event of the year will be the annual meeting with a theme-related seminar in Helsinki in October–November.

> *The Committee for the Future will improve its own work methods by developing its network-based activities, for example. The Committee proposes that various parties, which will exploit the results of technology foresight and assessment in their own activities, such as the Research Institute of the Finnish Economy (ETLA), the Labour Institute for Economic Research, the Finnish National Fund for Research and Development (SITRA), the National Research and Development Centre for Welfare and Health (STAKES), the Academy of Finland, the National Technology Agency (TEKES), the Finnish Academies of Technology, the Network Academies for Future Studies, the*

Science and Technology Policy Council of Finland, the Government Institute for Economic Research (VATT) and the Technical Research Centre of Finland (VTT), participate in preparing and implementing the activities to be undertaken during the chair period and nominate contact persons for this co-operation (and other joint activities with the Committee for the Future).

Helsinki, 13th December, 2000

The following persons participated in the decisive handling of this issue:

Chair: Martti Tiuri / National Coalition Party
Members: Jouni Backman / Social Democratic Party
Christina Gestrin / Swedish Peoples Party
Leena-Kaisa Harkimo / National Coalition Party
Leea Hiltunen / Christian Union
Ulla Juurola / Social Democratic Party
Reijo Kallio / Social Democratic Party
Kyösti Karjula / Centre Party
Markku Markkula / National Coalition Party
Rauha-Maria Mertjärvi / Green Party
Petri Neittaanmäki / Centre Party
Juha Rehula / Centre Party
Esko-Juhani Tennilä / Left-Wing Union
Pekka Vilkuna / Centre Party
Paula Tiihonen, Committee Counsellor, acted as the Committee secretary

Sources

Aho, H. & Leppänen, M. & Tamminen, T. 1998. Tieto on kuin ilo – se kasvaa jakamalla. [Knowledge is like joy—it increases through sharing.] INFO 1998:7. Helsinki University of Technology, Lifelong Learning Centre Dipoli. 30. Training for Information Service and Knowledge Resource Management 1997–98. Special assignment. Espoo, Finland.

Allee, V. 1997. The Knowledge Evolution. Expanding Organizational Intelligence. Butterworth-Heinemann. USA.

Autio, E. 2000. Alue, yrittäjyys ja talouskasvu: Vertailu Sophia Antipoliksen ja Espoon Otaniemen välillä. [Regions, Entrepreneurship and Economic Growth: Comparison between Sophia Antipolis, southern France, and the Espoo Otaniemi Area, Finland.] Article in a publication by Kostiainen, J. & Sotarauta, M. (eds.) 2000. Kaupungit innovatiivisina toimintaympäristöinä. [Urban Areas as Innovative Action Environments.] Finnish Association of Graduate Engineers TEK. Helsinki, Finland.

Autio-Tuuli, M. & Javanainen, P. & Kananen, A. & Rinne, M. 2000. Organisaation liiketoimintaympäristö – Tehoa business intelligence – toiminnalla. [Organisations' Business Environments—Increasing Efficiency through Business Intelligence Activities.] Helsinki University of Technology, Dipoli Training Centre. 32. Training for Information Service and Knowledge Resource Management 1999–00. Special assignment. Espoo, Finland

Botkin, J. W. & Elmandjra, M. & Malitza, M. 1981. New Challenges for Learning. Report for the Club of Rome. Espoo, Finland.

Bukowitz, W.R. & Williams, R.L. 1999. The Knowledge Management Fieldbook. Financial Times. Prentice Hall. UK.

Castells, M. 1996. The Rise of the Network Society—The Information Age: Economy, Society, and Culture. Blackwell Publishers.

Cohen, W. & Levinthal, D. 1990. Absorptive capacity: A new perspective on learning and innovation. Administrative Science Quarterly. 35.

Cortada, J.W. 1998. Rise of the Knowledge Worker. Butterworth-Heinemann. USA.

The Council of State's Report to Parliament Part 2: Skill and Fair Play—an Active and Responsible Finland. Helsinki, Finland. Parliamentary Office, 1997.

Csikszentmihalyi, M. 1996. Creativity, Flow and the Psychology of Discovery and Invention. New York: Harper Collins Publishers / Harper Perennial Division.

Davenport, T.H. & Prusak, L.1998: Working Knowledge. How Organizations Manage What They Know. Harvard Business School Press. Boston. Massachusetts.

Finland: A Society of Knowledge, Competence and Expertise. Helsinki, Finland. Science and Technology Policy Council of Finland, 1996.

From the Highways of Knowledge to the Sources of Creativity. A Human Approach to Information Societal Labour Policies. 1999. Ministry of Labour. Helsinki, Finland.

Handy, C. 1995. The Age of Unreason. Arrow Business Books. London.

Hautamäki, A. (ed.) 1996. Suomi teollisen ja tietoyhteiskunnan murroksessa. [Finland in the Transition from an Industrial to an Information Society.] SITRA 154.

Hintikka, K.A.1994. Virtuaalinen tila. Julkinen olohuone. [Virtual Space. A Public Living Room.] Helsinki, Finland.

Hintikka, K.A. 1999. Puheenvuorojen kirjasto 2. Keskustelua tietoyhteiskuntastrategiasta. [Statement Library 2. Discussion on Information Society Strategy.] SITRA 219. Helsinki, Finland.

Holma, A. & Lappalainen, K. & Pilkevaara. S. 1997. Näkymätön näkyväksi – tieto, osaaminen ja Knowledge Management. [Making the Invisible Visible—Knowlewdge, Competence and Knowledge Management.] INFO 1997:8. Helsinki University of Technology, Lifelong Learning Centre Dipoli. 29. Training for Information Service and Knowledge Resource Management 1996–97. Special assignment. Espoo, Finland.

Härmä, P. Tietotyöhön ihmisläheinen näkökulma. [Introducing the Human Aspect to Knowledge Work.] Helsingin Sanomat 7th May 2000.

Ilmakunnas, S. & Kiander, J. & Parkkinen. P. & Romppanen, A. 2000. Globalisaatio ja työn loppu? Talous ja työllisyys vuoteen 2030. [Globalisation and the End of Work? Economy and Employment until 2030.] Report by the Government Institute for Economic Research.

Jaspers, K. 1953. Introduction to Philosophy. Otava, Helsinki.

Noora Jokinen & Heli Suominen. Large Companies—Defenders of the Less-fortunate? Helsingin Sanomat 26th November 2000.

Kaivo-oja, J. & Kuusi, O. 1999. Arvioita ja analyysejä tietoyhteiskunnan työmarkkinoiden kehityspiirteistä Suomessa. [Assessments and Analyses of Labour Market Development in a Finnish information Society.] ESR publication 42/99. Helsinki, Finland.

Kalthoff, O. & Nonaka, I. & Nueno, P. 1997. The light and the shadow. How Breakthrough Innovation is Shaping European Business. Roland Berger Foundation. Cronwall.

Kasvi, J.J.J. & Vartiainen, M. (ed.) 2000. Organisaation muisti – Tieto työn tukena. [The Organisation's Memory—Knowledge as a Support to Work.] Edita. Helsinki, Finland.

Kilpi, E. 1999. Tietoperusteisen toiminnan haasteet yksilön ja yhteisön välisessä vuorovaikutuksessa. [Challenges of Knowledge-based Activities in Interaction Between Individuals and their Communities.] Työn Tuuli (Wind of Work) 2/1999.

Klein, A. 2000. Labour and Health, Future Challenges in Health and Safety Promotion. Publication article from: Professional Congress on The Future of Work. World Engineers' Convention. Expo 2000. Hannover, Germany.

Koivula, A. & Teikari, V. 1996. Pyramidi murenee – näkökulmia tietotyön prosessijohtamiseen. [The Pyramid is Crumbling—Perspectives to Process Management in Knowledge Work.] "Reaching the Future through Profitability" Programme. Hakapaino Oy. Helsinki, Finland.

Koski, J.T. 1999. Infoähky ja muita kirjoituksia oppimisesta, organisaatiosta ja tietoyhteiskunnasta. [Information Deluge and Other Articles on Learning, Organisation and Information Society.] Saarijärvi, Finland.

Kostiainen, J. 2000. Helsingin, Oulun ja Tampereen kaupunkiseudut innovatiivisina miljöinä. [The Urban Areas of Helsinki, Oulu and Tampere as Innovative Milieus.] Article in a publication by Kostiainen, J. & Sotarauta, M. (ed.) 2000. Kaupungit innovatiivisina toimintaympäristöinä. [Urban Areas as Innovative Action Environments.] The Finnish Association of Graduate Engineers TEK. Helsinki, Finland.

von Krogh, G. & Nonaka, I. & Nishiguchi, T. 2000. Knowledge Creation. A Source of Value. Macmillan Press Ltd. UK.

Kulkki, S. 1996. Knowledge Creation of Multinational Corporations. Knowledge Creation through Action. Helsinki School of Economics and Business Administration. Acta Universitatis Oeconomicae Helsingis. A-115, Helsinki, Finland.

Kuusi, O. 1986. Kohti osaamisen yhteiskuntaa. Artikkeleita tietoyhteiskunnan alueellisesta etenemisestä. Aluepoliittisia tutkimuksia ja selvityksiä 4/1986. [Toward a Society of Know-how. Articles on Regional Progress of Information Society. Research and Surveys on Regional Politics 4/1986.] The Ministry of the Interior, Department for Regional Development. Helsinki, Finland.

Kuusi, O. 1989. Osaaminen ja ammattirakenne. Uuden tietotekniikan vaikutuksia ammatteihin. [Know-how and Occupational Profiles. The Impact of New Information Technology on Occupations.] Economic Research Centre. Helsinki, Finland.

Kyrö, P. 1998. Yrittäjyyden tarinaa kertomassa. [A Story of Entrepreneurship.] Juva, Finland.

Kyrö, P. 2000. Entrepreneurship Education in a Virtual Learning Environment. Conference lecture: ICSB World Conference 2000. Entrepreneurial SMEs—Engines for Growth in the New Millennium 7–10 June 2000.

Lampikoski, K. & Suvanto, P. & Vahvaselkä, I. 1997. Markkinoinnin menestystekijät. [Success Factors in Marketing.] Porvoo, Finland.

Learning: The Treasure Within.1996. Report to UNESCO from the International Commission on Education for the Twenty-first Century. Paris, France: Unesco Publishing.

Levomäki, I . 1999. Arvojen moninaisuus tietoyhteiskunnassa. [The Variety of Values in Information Society.] SITRA.

Lipponen, P. 2000. Sähköisellä asioinnilla kilpailukykyisempään hallintoon. [Achieving More Efficient Administration Through E-business.] Edistys (Progress) 3/2000.

Liebowitz, J. & Beckman, T. 1998. Knowledge Organizations. What Every Manager Should Know. St. Lucie Press. USA.

Luukkainen, O. 2000. Opettaja vuonna 2010. Opettajien perus- ja täydennyskoulutuksen ennakointihankkeen [Teachers in 2010. Pre-survey for Teachers' Basic Education and Further Training Project] (OPEPRO) Report 15. Final report. National Board of Education. ESR. Helsinki, Finland.

Markkula, M. & Suurla, R. 1997. Elinikäisen oppimisen hyvät käytännöt. [Good Practices in Lifelong Learning.] Second amended edition. Appendix to Lifelong Learning Committee Report (1997:14). Helsinki, Finland.

Markkula, M. & Suurla, R. 1998. Passion to Learn. Benchmarking Good Lifelong Learning Practice. IACEE Report No 9/1998.

Markkula, M. 1999. Tulevaisuusvaliokunta luo polkuja menestykseen. [The Committee for the Future Opens New Paths to Success.] Futura 4/99. Future Research Association.

Nahapiet, J. & Ghoshal, S. 1998. Social capital, intellectual capital and the organizational advantage. Academy of Management Review. 23 (2).

Niiniluoto, I. 1988. Informaatio, tieto ja yhteiskunta. Filosofinen käsiteanalyysi. [Information, Knowledge and Society. A Philosophic Conceptual Analysis.] The State's Printing Centre. Helsinki, Finland

Negroponte, N. 2000. Questions and Answers. Nicholas Negroponte on Following Your Passion. Training, May 2000.

Nonaka, I. 1991. The Knowledge-Creating Company. Harvard Business Review. November—December.

Nonaka, I. & Takeuchi, H. 1995. The Knowledge-Creating Company. Oxford University press. New York.

Nonaka, I & Konno, N. 1998. The Concept of "Ba": Building a Foundation for Knowledge Creation. California Management Review. Vol. 40, No 3.

Nonaka, I & Umemoto, K. & Sasaki, K. 1998. Managing and Measuring Knowledge in Organizations. (von Krogh, G. & Roos, J. & Kleine, D. Knowing in Firms. Understanding, Managing and Measuring Knowledge.) SAGE Publications. UK.

Nonaka, I., Toyama, R, & Konno, N. 2000. SECI, Ba and Leadership: A Unified Model of Dynamic Knowledge Creation. Long Range Planning. Vol. 33, 5–34. 2000.

Otala, L. 1999. Oppijohtaminen, 2000-luvun johtamishaaste. [Learning Management—A Leadership Challenge for the 21st century.] Aristos 2/1999. Skills Academy Ltd. Helsinki, Finland.

Painspots in the Future of Work (Committee for the Future and Government Institute for Economic Research, 10/2000)

Pehrman, T. 2000. Oppiva johtajuus. Energiaa työyhteisöön ja liiketoimintaan. [Learning Leadership. Energy for Co-operation and Business Activities.] University of Jyväskylä. MBA research.

Polanyi, M. 1958. Personal Knowledge. Towards a Post-Critical Philosophy. Routledge. London.

Polanyi, M. 1966. The Tacit Dimension. London.

Raivola, R. & Vuorensyrjä, M. 1998. Osaaminen tietoyhteiskunnassa – selvitys kansallisen tietoyhteiskuntastrategian uudistamisen taustaksi. [Competence and Expertise in the Information Society—A Survey for Reforming the National Information Society Strategy.] SITRA 180. Helsinki, Finland.

Rask, M. & Eela, R. & Heikkerö, T. & Neuvonen, A. 1999. Teknologian arviointi, arvot ja osallistuminen – kokemuksia geenitekniikka-arvioista. [Technology Assessments, Values and Participation—Experiences on Gene Technological Assessments.] VTT. Espoo, Finland.

Rogers, E. 1983. Diffusion of Innovations. Third Edition. The Free Press. New York.

Rogers, E. & Shoemaker, F. 1971. Communication of Innovations. Second Edition. The Free Press. New York.

Savolainen, V-A. & Himanen, P. 1995. Kohtaamisyhteiskunta. [A Society of Encounter.] Edita. Helsinki, Finland.

Skyrme, D.J. 1999. Knowledge Networking. Creating the Collaborative Enterprise. Butterworth-Heinemann. USA.

Ståhle, P. & Grönroos, M. 1999. Knowledge Management – tietopääoma yrityksen kilpailutekijänä. [Knowledge Management—Knowledge Assets as a Success Factor for Companies.] Porvoo, Finland.

Stewart, T. 1997. Intellectual Capital. Nicholas Brealey Publishing. London.

Suurla, R. 1998. Laadukas elämä ja yhdessä oppiminen. [High-quality Life and Learning Together.] Aristos 1/1998.

Suurla, R. & Markkula, M. & Finnish Leonardo Centre. 1999. Methods and Tools for Effective Dissemination. A Guide to the Dissemination of the Results of International Educational Projects. Jyväskylä, Finland.

Sveiby, K.E. 1997. The New Organizational Wealth. San Francisco.

Teikari, V. 1999. Yhteiskunnan muutos ja yliopistoyksikön selviytymishaasteet. [Societal Change and Coping Challenges Encountered by University Units.] Adult Education 1/99.

Tiihonen, S. 2000. Miten nostaa valtioneuvoston hallintakapasiteettia tietoyhteiskunnassa? [How to Increase the Government's Administration Management Capacity in an Information Society?] Administrative Research 4/2000. Helsinki, Finland.

Tuomi, I. 1999. Corporate Knowledge. Theory and Practice of Intelligent Organizations. Metaxis. Helsinki, Finland.

TuVM 1/1997 vp Report by the Committee for the Future on the Council of State (Government) Report Part 1 "Finland and the Future of Europe"

TuVM 1/1998 vp Report by the Committee for the Future on the Council of State (Government) Report part 2 "Skill and Fair Play—an Active and Responsible Finland"

TuVL 1/2000 vp Statement of the Committee for the Future of Council of State report on the Commission communication

Wickens, P. 1999. Energise your Enterprise. Macmillan Press Ltd. UK.

Wiig, K. 1997. Knowledge Management: Where Did It Come From And Where Will It Go? Expert Systems with Applications, Pergamon Press / Elsevier, Vol.14.

Wikström, S. & Normann, R. & Annell, B. & Ekvall, G. & Skärvad, P-H. 1994. Knowledge & Value.

Väyrynen, R. 1999. Suomi avoimessa maailmassa. [Finland in an Open World. Globalisation and its Consequences.] SITRA. Helsinki, Finland.

Yli-Renko, H. Autio, E. & Sapienza, H. 2000. Social capital, knowledge acquisition, and competitive advantage in technology-based new firms. Submitted to the Strategic Management Journal.

Unprinted sources

Interviews conducted by Project Manager Riitta Suurla:

Interview with Klaus Frösén in Helsinki, 6th July 2000.

Interview with Merja Karivalo in Espoo, 6th August 2000.

Interview with Esko Kilpi in Espoo, 8th February 2000.

Interview with Osmo Kuusi in Helsinki, 22nd June 2000.

Interview with John Lorriman in Espoo, 7th August 2000.

Interview with Ikujiro Nonaka in Helsinki, 21st July 2000.

Interview with Olli Mustajärvi in Helsinki, 26th July 2000.

Interview with Anja Stenius in Helsinki, 8th March 2000.

Interview with Pirjo Ståhle in Helsinki, 19th April 2000.

Interview with Auni-Marja Vilavaara in Helsinki, 22 June 2000.

Other unprinted sources:

A journey report from the USA by Kimmo Halme, 2000.

Järvinen, E-M. 2000. Yleissivistävä teknologiakasvatus. [Technological Education for General Educational Purposes.] A Lecture Paper for Information and Training Occasions on Technological Education ("Technological Education - NOW!") Ylivieska and Oulu, Finland, 16th and 23rd March 2000.

Lecture by Ikujiro Nonaka at the Espoo seminar on 22nd June 1998.

Lecture by Terhi Ogbeide in Helsinki, 5th January 2000.